"I Would Still Be Drowned in Tears":
Spiritualism in Abraham Lincoln's White House

4/25/14

To Loren,
For everything & much
Love.

Michelle L. Hamilton

Michelle L. Hamilton

Vanderblǔmen Publications
P.O. Box 626
La Mesa, CA 91944

Library of Congress Cataloging-in-Publication Data

Hamilton, Michelle L.
I would still be drowned in tears: Spiritualism in Abraham Lincoln's White House / by Michelle L. Hamilton

ISBN: 978-0-9644304-6-4

1. Lincoln, Abraham, 1809-1865—Religion. 2. Lincoln, Mary Todd, 1818-1862—Religion. 3. Spiritualism—United States—History—19th century. 4. Spirituality—Unites States—Case studies. 5. Presidents—Religious life—United States—Case Studies. 6. Presidents—United States—Biography.

To Mom and Dad

In loving memory of

Carolyn Winer,
Jennifer Lindell,
and Elijah Blum

*"For of such is the kingdom
of heaven."*

Acknowledgements

I would like to thank the following who have helped me complete this project. This would never have been created without the inspiration and guidance that Dr. Edward J. Blum provided to me from the very first day that I started at San Diego State University. From my days as an undergraduate to the completion of my thesis, Ed has served as not only my professor, but as my mentor and my friend. During a difficult time, you allowed me to be there for you and your family. I am indebted to Dr. William Weeks whose advice shaped the content and direction of this book and who kept reminding me to be have the courage to stand up for my convictions. Thanks must also be given to Dr. Susan Calyeff who saw the potential in this project.

Without the professional expertise and kindness of the following people and institutions who welcomed me into their midst during my research. At the Abraham Lincoln Presidential Library and Museum, James M. Cornelius made me and my mother feel welcome and graciously took time to share his insights on the Lincolns' religious beliefs and marriage. Michelle Gantz, archivist at Lincoln Memorial Library and Museum kindly answered my queries and provided me with copies of hard to find sources. Jerry A. McCoy librarian of the Peabody Room, Georgetown Neighborhood Library helped me locate information on the Laurie family. Megan Halsband at the Library of Congress graciously helped me locate illusive copies of *The Religio-Philosophical Journal*. Finally, I wish to thank the staff of the Lincoln Library Sangamon Valley Collection for their kind assistance in accessing the *Daily Illinois State Journal* and the *Daily Illinois State Register*.

I am deeply thankful to my Mom and Dad for supporting me throughout my education, supporting my passion for the Civil War, and for putting up with all of my books. I wish also to express my gratitude to Amber Tiffany-Furuya and Caitlin Wion for their support and friendship. To Pam Brown who keeps Mary Lincoln alive. To my friend and editor, Glenna Bloemen who fine tuned my writing. Finally I must thank Carolyn Winer, Jennifer Lindell, and Elijah Blum who lived life to the fullest regardless of the time they were given. The world is a better place because they were here and heaven is a better place because they are there.

Introduction

"Was he more superstitious than the people of his age?

In February 1863 a group of individuals gathered at a residence in Georgetown a suburb of Washington, D.C. These people had gathered to take part in a Spiritualist séance. The spirits were ready for the party and demonstrated their power by causing a piano to levitate. Amused by the incident, one of the guests decided to climb up on the piano to see if he could prevent it from levitating. This did not dissuade the spirits and the piano continued to rise up and down as the piano was being played. While the scene might have the aura of fantasy, the séance did occur and the person that decided to sit on the piano was none other than President Abraham Lincoln. Brought to the séance by his wife Mary, the President was intrigued by the events that he saw that night, but it was not his first séance and it would not be his last.

That Abraham Lincoln attended Spiritualist séances during the Civil War horrified the President's friends. Rushing to the aide of their friend after his death, they claimed that the President only attended a few séances to humor his mental unstable wife. John G. Nicolay claimed, "I never knew of his attending a séance of Spiritualists at the White House or elsewhere." (1) Historians have taken this statement as definitive proof that the claims made by Spiritualists were exaggerations. Yet, they neglect Nicolay's further statement. "Of course, I have no doubt that Mr. Lincoln like a great many other men, *might* have had some curiosity as to spiritualism, and *might* have attended some of the séances solely out of curiosity…*if* President Lincoln ever attended séances…it was with this same feeling of curiosity," Nicolay admitted. (2)

President Abraham Lincoln has become an iconic figure in American history, a larger than life character that stares down at us from the Lincoln Memorial and from movie theater screens. For modern historians a figure of such epic would never have willingly participated in a belief system which proclaimed that it was possible to communicate with the spirits of the dead. This narrative have influenced several generations of Lincoln scholars who have concluded that President Lincoln's attendance at Spiritualist séances during the Civil War was his attempt to humor his grieving—and likely crazy—wife.

While this interpretation has become ingrained in the historiography, it is not supported by the primary sources. Even Lincoln's law partner, William Herndon, was forced to admit in 1885, "Mr. Lincoln was in some phases of his nature very, very superstitious; and it may be—it is quite probable that he in his gloom, sadness, fear, and despair, invoked the spirits of the dead to reveal to him the cause of his states of gloom, sadness, fear and despair. He craved light from all intelligences to flash his way to the unknown future of his life." (3)

Despite such statements, historians have dismissed Abraham and Mary Lincoln's interest in Spiritualism. Referring to President Lincoln's involvement with Spiritualism, religious scholar Stephan Mansfield declared, "The entire episode stained Lincoln's reputation and confused the issue of his religious beliefs for generations after, and it had all come from Mary's tortured grieving and her insistence upon pushing beyond the boundaries of her Presbyterian faith." (4) Mansfield's statement represents the typical scholarly reaction to Mary Lincoln's belief in Spiritualism.

Spiritualism was a powerful force in the religious landscape of nineteenth-century American, yet scholars have struggled with incorporating Spiritualist belief into the narrative of American history. One major exception is historian Catherine L. Albanese whose groundbreaking study, *A Republic of Mind and Spirit: A Cultural History of American Metaphysical Religion*, demonstrated that metaphysical religion (which included Spiritualism) has been part of the religious landscape since the Colonial era. (5) According to Albanese, "metaphysical forms of religion have privileged the mind in forms that include reason but move beyond it to intuition, clairvoyance, and its relatives such as 'revelation' and 'higher guidance.'" (6) Since the claims of Spiritualism are hard to definitely prove, scholars have struggled with accepting the testimony of Spiritualists within the historical narrative. Despite Albanese's work, reticence has remained towards the subject and has affected how historians have addressed the followers of Spiritualism.

No follower of Spiritualism has been more controversial than Mary Lincoln. For her detractors, Mary Lincoln's interest in Spiritualism is viewed as conclusive evidence of her mental instability. (7) President Abraham Lincoln, the traditional narrative contends, was dragged unwillingly to Spiritualist séances in an attempt to protect his mentally fragile wife. "Presently she [Mary Lincoln] became the victim of spiritualists, who claimed they could put her in touch with her darling lost boy…The president attended at least one of those [séances], not out of any belief in spiritualism, but in a desire to see who was preying on his wife's mental instability," historian David H. Donald intoned. (8) Despite the primary sources that commented on Abraham and Mary Lincolns' metaphysical beliefs and their involvement in Spiritualism, historians have failed to examine this facet of their lives. In recent years, Wayne C. Temple, Allen C. Guelzo, and Stephen Mansfield have published books that examined Abraham Lincoln's faith. Yet, all have downplayed Abraham Lincoln's attendance at Spiritualist séances during the Civil War.

This tradition has neglected Abraham and Mary Lincoln's life-long interest and belief in metaphysical religious practices. A product of their Kentucky childhood, the Lincolns shared a common belief in dreams and omens which they incorporated into their Christian faith. "The impressions of the spirit were not lost on Lincoln either, whose sensitive nature, eager mind, and depression-ravaged psyche made him tender to—even eager for—invisible realities. During his lifetime he experienced dreams, omens, visions, and revelatory occurrences of nearly every kind, and they did not decrease with age," Stephen Mansfield noted. (9)

While President Abraham Lincoln's metaphysical beliefs are generally viewed sympathetically, Mary Lincoln's similar beliefs are nearly universally condemned. Writer Stephen Mansfield while discussing Abraham Lincoln's "heartfelt" and "wise" approach to religion referred to Mary Lincoln's belief in Spiritualism as a tragedy. (10) Mansfield was not the only person who characterized Mary Lincoln's reliance on Spiritualism as a character flaw. "I wish…that she had not become involved with spiritualism after Willie's death. It would have provided her professional detractors with a few less redoubts for attack," novelist Irving Stone bemoaned. (11)

Thus, the scholarship of Abraham and Mary Lincolns' interest in Spiritualism during the Civil War has been divided between the pro and anti Spiritualist camp. Only three published works have detailed the Lincoln's involvement with Spiritualism. Susan B. Martinez's, *The Psychic Life of Abraham Lincoln*; Troy Taylor's, *The Haunted President: The History, Hauntings & Supernatural Life of Abraham Lincoln;* and, Christopher Kiernan Coleman's, *The Paranormal Presidency of Abraham Lincoln* presents the paranormal aspects of the Lincolns' lives.

The purpose of this thesis is to examine Abraham and Mary Lincoln's interest in Spiritualism during the Civil War in the context of the culture in which they lived. As historian Jay Monaghan questioned, "Such stories, if true, should be viewed in the light of President Lincoln's time. Was he more superstitious than the people of his age, and does it necessarily follow that he believed in the philosophy of spiritualism with its recognized 'mediums' under 'control' of spirits who spoke through them and sometimes came visibly into the séance chamber?" (12) Indeed such stories suggest that President Abraham Lincoln's continued attendance at séances during the Civil War illustrate that, contrary to traditional depictions, he shared an interest in Spiritualism with his wife.

Through an examination of memoirs, letters, diary entries, and newspaper articles, my research shows that the Lincolns shared an interest in metaphysical religion which they entwined with their Christian faith. Abraham and Mary Lincoln's attendance at Spiritualist séances during the dark days of the Civil War was a culmination of their shared metaphysical beliefs and should be viewed within the context of 19th-century American culture.

Part One

"In the old days God and His angels came to men in their sleep"

February 5, 1862 had been planned as Abraham and Mary Lincolns' finest moment in the White House. After months of costly renovation, the Lincolns were presenting to the nation, an Executive Mansion that befitted the American presidency. (13) Rather than basking in the glory of their accomplishments, though, the Lincolns spent the majority of the evening nursing their son. For two weeks, 11-year-old Willie Lincoln had been critically ill with typhoid fever. Concerned over her son's condition, Mary had considered canceling the reception, but the family's physician had soothed the anxious mother by proclaiming that there was no cause for alarm. (14) The boy was improving, and would recover shortly the doctor concluded. Assured that Willie was on the mend, President Abraham Lincoln ruled that the reception would go on as scheduled, but the dance that had been planned as part of the evening's festivities would be canceled out of respect for the sick boy. (15)

With the reception going on as scheduled Abraham and Mary Lincoln prepared to welcome their guests. Just as the carriages carrying the elegantly dressed guests began to arrive at the White House, Willie's condition began to rapidly deteriorate. (16) Sitting at Willie's bedside that night, Elizabeth Keckly, (17) the First Lady's seamstress and confidant wrote in her memoir, "The brilliance of the scene could not dispel the sadness that rested upon the face of Mrs. Lincoln." (18)

Abraham Lincoln was also anguished by the turn of events. A woman who attended the reception recalled, "A sadder face than that of the President I have rarely seen. He was receiving at the large door of the East Room, speaking to the people as they came, but feeling so deeply that he spoke of what he felt and thought, instead of welcoming the guests. To General Fremont he at once said that his son was very ill and he feared for the result." (19)

The sadness the Lincolns felt that night remained as the days slowly wore on. Instead of improving, as the doctor had initially promised, Willie according to Keckly "grew weaker and more shadow-like." (20) Fifteen days after the White House reception, Willie succumbed and died on February 20, 1862. (21) The death of their child emotionally and physically devastated Abraham and Mary Lincoln. While the President grieved in private, Mary fell into a fit of hysterics and was confined to her bedroom. (22) During their mourning, the Lincolns began to attend Spiritualist séances. The Lincolns were extremely private about their personal lives and a number of documents have been destroyed by the Lincoln family in attempt to protect their privacy. (23) However, following a careful study of primary sources, I have come to the conclusion that the Lincolns both shared an interest in metaphysical beliefs culminating in their interest in Spiritualism during the Civil War.

Historians have neglected this aspect of Abraham Lincoln's life, instead asserting that the President's involvement in Spiritualism stemmed from his attempt to humor his mentally unstable wife. (24) Ignored by historians was that throughout his life, Abraham Lincoln expressed his belief in the prophecy of dreams. This belief in the unknown made the President open to Spiritualism after Willie's death. This added a new dimension to the religious life of the Lincoln family which reflected the blending of Christianity and metaphysics during the 19th-century. To fully understand the appeal Spiritualism held for Abraham and Mary Lincoln, we must examine their life through the prism of their metaphysical beliefs.

Chapter One

"A Religious Oddity"

Abraham Lincoln was born on February 12, 1809 in a simple log cabin three miles south of Hodgenville, Kentucky to Thomas and Nancy Hanks Lincoln. (25) At the time of his birth his parents were members of the Little Mount Baptist Church. As the issue of slavery began to slowly divide the Union, the issue also divided his parents' church which resulted in their decision to leave and join the Separate Baptists whose members predominately held anti-slavery beliefs. (26) Despite being raised in an evangelical household, Abraham did not embrace the strict faith of his parents. Throughout his life and even into the present day, Lincoln has remained, in the words of writer Stephen Mansfield, "a religious oddity." (27)

Further complicating Abraham Lincoln's relationship with religion was his culture's reliance on metaphysical practices. Abraham Lincoln lived in a culture that embraced a number of metaphysical beliefs since the Colonial era. A product of the Renaissance, the European immigrants who flocked to the New World for religious freedom and economic opportunities brought to America metaphysical beliefs. (28) In a time where health care was virtually non-existent, Abraham's community practiced folk magic to cure aliments and ward off illness. To conservative Christians, this looked like witchcraft and future Lincoln biographers struggled with his cultures reliance of magic.

William Herndon wrote in his biography of Abraham Lincoln, "Although gay, prosperous, and light-hearted, these people were brimming over with superstition. It was at once their food and drink. They believed in the baneful influence of witches, pinned their faith in the curative powers of wizards in dealing with sick animals, and shot the image of a witch with a silver ball to break the spell she was supposed to have over human beings." (29) In the 1880's, John Nicolay, Lincoln's presidential secretary, could barely hide his disdain for the culture in which the future president was raised in. Nicolay wrote in his biography, "The belief in witchcraft had long ago passed away with the smoke of the fagots from old and New England, but it survived far into this century in Kentucky and the lower halves of Indiana and Illinois—touched with a peculiar tinge of African magic." (30)

It was this complexity of beliefs that surrounded Lincoln during his childhood. This would have a profound impact on Lincoln for the remainder of his life. While he was able to shake the rigid Christianity of his parents, he would never shake his metaphysical beliefs. The religious and political issues that were slowly ripping the country apart also influenced where the Abraham grew up. Frustrated by the growing power of the slave holder elite and discouraged by the lack of available farm land, Thomas Lincoln decided to move his family to the free state of Indiana in 1816. (31) Arriving in Indiana, the elder Lincoln quickly joined the Pigeon Creek Baptist Church where he served his new congregation by assisting in the construction of the church building. (32)

In 1828, Abraham Lincoln got a glimpse of the outside world when he was hired to take a flatboat stocked with goods to the market in New Orleans. (33) While in New Orleans, Lincoln was exposed to the vibrant culture of the city, including an introduction to the Voudou religion. Abraham did not stay in the city long, but retuned in 1831 accompanied by his cousin, Dennis Hanks. (34) In the years following President Lincoln's death, Hanks recalled that while in New Orleans Lincoln visited a Voudou fortune teller. (35) According to the story, the Voudou priestess informed Lincoln that he would become the President of the United States. (36) According to Hanks, the Voudou seer exclaimed, "You will be president, and all the Negroes will be free!" (37) Hanks eventually retracted his claim, asserting, "I Don't [k]Now whether he got his fortune told or Not." (38) This exposure to Voudou would have added another demission of the metaphysical practices which Abraham Lincoln encountered during his youth.

Upon reaching his maturity, Abraham Lincoln left his family and moved to the Illinois boomtown of New Salem where he abandoned Christianity. Finally, free from his father, Lincoln embraced his independence with a relish. "By the time he ambled into New Salem, he had rejected the wildness of camp meeting religion and found it hard to hide his disdain for most preachers," historian Steven Mansfield noted. (39) In New Salem, Lincoln found a group of like-minded companions. Like a rebellious teenager, Lincoln seemed to relish shocking the townspeople with his denunciations of Christianity and the clergy. (40)

Despite his abandonment of his Christian heritage, Lincoln was still surrounded by metaphysical practices. Settled largely by emigrants from Kentucky and Indiana, the residents of New Salem brought with them their metaphysical beliefs. (41) Denton Offutt, who had introduced Lincoln to New Salem, advertised his skills as a "horse whisperer" after leaving the settlement. (32) Though there is little scholarship on the metaphysical practices in New Salem, Offutt likely helped his neighbors' horses and livestock by treating them with folk cures while he lived in the settlement.

It was in this religious climate that Abraham Lincoln came to maturity. From his birth, Lincoln entered a community that mixed Christianity and metaphysical religion to protect their body and soul. As he entered adulthood, Lincoln developed a firm belief in the power of dreams and omens to tell the future. In 1832, Lincoln admitted to a friend that he was, "always was superstitious". (43) While Lincoln was growing to maturity and developing his metaphysical beliefs, a young woman in Lexington, Kentucky was also developing her own metaphysical beliefs.

Chapter Two

"Howdy, Mr. Jay"

Mary Ann Todd was born on December 13, 1818 to Robert and Eliza Parker Todd in Lexington, Kentucky. (44) The Todds were Presbyterians and raised their children under the rites of the church as members of the McCord Presbyterian Church. (45) The family celebrated their Scottish ancestors who had been banished from their homeland after refusing to convert to the Church of England and submitting to the rule of King Charles II during the 1600's. (46) By the 19th-century, the Todds' faith had come to represent both a personal faith and the clans' commitment to family tradition.

Following the death of her mother, Mary's father re-married in an attempt to provide a mother for his children. (47) Robert's bride, Elizabeth "Betsy" Humphreys Todd proved unprepared for the daunting task of filling the maternal void left by the death of her predecessor. (48) As adults, Mary's sisters asserted that Betsey Todd was particularly hard on Mary compared to the other children from her husband's first marriage. (49) Elizabeth Edwards, Mary's oldest sister, concluded that "She [Mary] had a Step Mother with whom she did not agree." (50) Betsy

Todd failed in uniting the blended family, making the house miserable for the children of Robert's first marriage. To fill the void left by her mother's death, Mary turned to her father's slave, Mammy Sally, who served as the nanny to the numerous Todd children. (51) Through the ministrations of Sally, Mary was introduced to the emotionalism of Methodist church services and African American metaphysical beliefs. (52)

After returning from Methodist church services, the pious Mammy Sally would entertain Mary and her sisters with stories about the devil and hell. "We shivered," remembered Elizabeth Todd, Mary's cousin, and the girls would clamp their hands over their ears during Mammy Sally's stories. (53) While Mary's sisters and cousin were horrified by Mammy Sally's tales, Mary was intrigued. "Mary was so fascinated with Mammy's descriptions of his Satanic majesty that she made her repeat it time and time again, although we knew it by heart," Elizabeth remembered. (54) In an attempt to get Mary and her siblings to behave, Mammy Sally solemnly informed the children that jay birds were the devil's messengers.

According to Mammy Sally, jay birds traveled to hell every Friday to inform Satan on the weekly misdeeds of the Todd children. Mary was unimpressed by this story and upon seeing a jay bird in her family's garden the girl would chant, "Howdy, Mr. Jay. You are a tell-tale-tell. You play the spy each day, then carry tales to hell." (55)

Metaphysical belief in the United States at this time was not simply confined to poor frontier folk or African slaves. Julia Dent, the future wife of Ulysses S. Grant, was a firm believer in metaphysics. Born in Missouri, as a child, Julia Dent Grant was exposed to metaphysical beliefs from her family's slaves. For the rest of her life, Julia was a firm believer in premonitions, omens, and the power of dreams to foretell the future. (56) Thus, with her family's Presbyterian faith and the metaphysical beliefs of her culture, Mary Todd came to maturity surrounded by a complex array of religious beliefs and traditions. Like many Southern girls during the antebellum period, Mary joined an established church after her twelfth birthday. (57)

Instead of embracing the evangelical faith of her parents, Mary rebelled by being confirmed into the Episcopal Church. (58) Mary's decision to become an Episcopalian must have raised a stir within her tradition bound family. The Todds and their in-laws were deeply committed to their Presbyterian faith, as the will of Mary's step-grandmother, Mary Humphreys, illustrates. According to the dictates of the will one of her slaves, John, was to be educated and trained for the ministry and was to be emancipated after her death. Following his emancipation John was to be sent to Liberia "to make Scotch Presbyterians of the heathen." (59) Needless to say the Todds and their extended family where firmly committed to their faith.

No explanation for Mary Todd's choice to turn away from the faith of her ancestors has survived. It is just as likely that Mary's choice to join the Episcopal Church had nothing to do with religion, but was her way of rebelling against her step-mother. The hours spent in worship away from her parents granted Mary a period of relative freedom from the rule of Betsey Todd. Mary reveled in being rebellious, as seen in her bravado towards Mammy Sally's stories. It is completely in character that Mary Todd decided to be rebellious in her choice of religious beliefs. While Mary rejected the faith of her family, she did not reject the metaphysical beliefs that were part of her culture—just like her future husband.

Chapter Three

"Of Such Is the Kingdom of Heaven"

By 1840, Mary Todd was pushed to the limits of her endurance with her step-mother Betsey Todd and as a result moved to Springfield, Illinois to live with her married sister Elizabeth Edwards. (60) Mary seized the opportunity to escape from her disapproving stepmother and welcomed the chance of finding a husband during the social season in Illinois's new state capital. Upon her arrival in Illinois, Mary began attending St. Paul's Episcopal Church. (61) Mary's action upon moving to Springfield illustrated that her commitment to the Episcopal Church had blossomed into a true belief as she matured. At this time, though, Mary had more on her mind than just religion.

That the object of Mary Todd's heart happened to be a poor and uncouth lawyer named Abraham Lincoln shocked and dismayed her sister who saw it as her role as a chaperone to properly marry her sister off. Arriving in Springfield in 1840 to pursue a career as a lawyer, Abraham Lincoln was viewed as an up and coming politician in the state's Whig Party. Despite possessing a promising future, Mary Todd's family objected to the couple's relationship. Elizabeth Edwards had married well by Southern standards, having chosen the son of Illinois's third governor to be her husband. (62) Shocked by Mary's choice, she did everything in her power to break up the couple, briefly succeeding in 1841 when the couple separated for a year. In this battle of wills, the willful Mary Todd prevailed and married Abraham Lincoln on November 4, 1842. (63)

During the time that Abraham and Mary Lincoln's courtship occurred, America was being swept up by a religious revival known as the "Second Great Awakening." During this period, there was little evidence to suggest that Abraham and Mary Lincoln showed any interest in the evangelical furor that was sweeping around them. Instead, Mary Lincoln occupied her time assisting with her new husband's political career and becoming a mother. Out of the Second Great Awaking, Spiritualism emerged in 1848. Spiritualism left an indelible mark on America's religious and political landscape.

In the spring of 1848, the small farming village of Hydesville, New York became the birth place of a religious movement that would captivate the nation. It all began when 14-year-old Maggie and her 11-year-old sister Kate Fox announced to their neighbors that their house was haunted. The Fox sisters explained that they were able to communicate with the ghost through a series of knocks emanating from the walls. (64) Intrigued, local residents flocked to the Fox residence where it soon became clear that the activity in the Fox house increased when Maggie and Kate were in attendance and the girls quickly claimed that they possessed the ability to communicate with the spirit.

Out of these humble origins, Spiritualism emerged. Spiritualist belief is simple, as historian Barbara Weisberg explained, "Instead, the state commonly called death is only a transition period, a shedding of the body, and the spirits of individuals not only survive beyond the grave but also communicate from the other side." (65) For those who did not possess the gift to speak with the dead, mediums emerged to transmit the messages from the spirits. (66) At its peak, Spiritualism claimed two million believers within the United States. (67)

To capitalize on their new found fame, Maggie and Kate traveled throughout the North showcasing their talents by holding demonstrations in sold-out theaters and by performing intimate séances in the parlors of their converts. Spiritualism's spread was dramatic. LaRoy Sunderland a Boston Spiritualist recorded that in 1850, "there was not one family known throughout the New England states, where responses from the spirit world had been made to questions put by mortals," yet within a year there were "a thousand mediums, witnessed in every state." (68) In 1870, Emma Hardinge reflected on the growth of Spiritualism, "The ball once set rolling…sped on with an impetus which soon transcended the power of the press, pulpit or public to arrest, despite of every force that was brought to bear against us." (69) Though the Fox sisters were the founders of the new religion, Spiritualism quickly surpassed them.

Wherever Maggie and Kate Fox traveled in the North, Spiritualist communities were established in their wake. (70) The spread of Spiritualism offered middle-class women with the opportunity of perusing a respectable career in an era where the numbers of jobs open to women were limited. Besides offering women employment, Spiritualism also proved to be an appealing doctrine for women who used the new faith as an outlet for their grief following the death of a husband or child. (71) Besides providing religious and emotional solace to the bereaved, Spiritualism, because of its lack of structured hierarchy offered women an active leadership role within the religious movement. This allowed women the freedom to lead séances where they not only passed along messages from the dearly departed, but also expound on social and political issues.

Under the umbrella of Spiritualism, the movement granted women an active voice in social and political reform movements under the protection that they were not voicing their own personal views, but that of the spirits. (72) The Spiritualist medium's parlor made a perfect place for socially active women to expound on issues such as abolition and women's rights within the protection of the domestic circle. (73) Naturally, this doctrine appealed to Northern social activists with feminist and abolitionists making up a significant number of Spiritualists. (74) Though embraced by social activists, the idea of women lecturing during the antebellum era horrified conservative Americans. One man even went so far as to declare that he would rather see his beloved daughter dead than see her join the "female croakers" giving lectures. (75)

Despite Spiritualism's growth in the North, Spiritualism was never as popular in the South. (76) Though Spiritualist circles did emerge in the South before the Civil War, particularly in New Orleans for the large part, the conservative Southerners could not abide with a religion that counted abolitionists and feminists within its ranks. (77) Despite meeting resistance in the South, Spiritualism did find a foothold in one Southern city—the nation's capital, Washington, D.C. (78)

Spiritualism came to the White House during the administration of Franklin Pierce. The tragic life of Franklin Pierce's wife, Jane, rivaled that of Mary Lincoln. By the time Franklin Pierce had been elected president in 1852, the Pierces' had already lost two of their three sons. (79) The Pierces' remaining son Benjamin, called Benny, by his doting parents became his mother's pride and joy. Sadly, Benny's time with his parents proved to be short. While traveling with his parents to Washington, D.C. the 11-year-old was killed in a train accident. His parents had emerged from the accident badly bruised, but otherwise uninjured, while Benny's head had been severed by falling luggage. (80)

During her time in the White House, Jane Pierce remained largely secluded from public affairs earning her the nickname "the shadow of the White House." (81) Shut away in the White House, Jane Pierce spent her time writing letters to Benny. "I do not know how to go on without you—you were my comfort dear—far more than you thought…Oh! you were indeed 'a part of mine and your father's heart.' When I have told you dear boy how much you depended on me, and felt that you could not do without me—I did not say too how much I depended on you," Jane Pierce wrote. (82) In 1853, Jane Pierce invited Maggie Fox to the White House to conduct a séance. (83). Following this séance, Spiritualism would have to wait another 9 years before it would return to the White House.

While she followed the tenets of the Episcopal Church, Mary Lincoln also exhibited a tendency to be swayed by metaphysical incidents. Mary shared this trait with her husband as both Abraham and Mary believed in omens and dreams as a fortune telling device. (84) Abraham Lincoln's superstitious nature was well known to his contemporaries. William Herndon declared that his law partner had "a superstitious view of life," which was as prominent in him "like the thin blue vein through the whitest marble." (85)

A century and a half later, Abraham Lincoln is still criticized for his superstitious nature. "For all his greatness Abraham Lincoln was of course human. Among his foibles were a tendency to melancholy, a sense of fatalism, a touch of superstition from his frontier upbringing," wrote noted paranormal skeptic Joe Nickel. (86) Rather than viewing Abraham and Mary Lincoln's superstitions as a character flaw, it is important to place their beliefs within their culture which embraced metaphysical beliefs such as Spiritualism and Mesmerism.

As a newlywed, Mary Lincoln tried Mesmerism, to cure her chronic migraine headaches. (87) Based on the theories of the eighteenth-century Austrian healer, Anton Mesmer, Mesmerism argued that everything and everyone was composed of an electro-magnetic fluid. Illness was caused, according to Mesmer, due to an imbalance of the fluid. This could be easily cured by mesmerists who placed their patients into a trance and then waved their hands over their patient's body which realigned the patient's fluid. (88) An unexpected side-effect from being mesmerized was that during trances many patients claimed that they had seen spirits and had gained clairvoyant powers. (89)

By the 1840's, Mesmerism had gathered a large following in the United States. (90) Mesmerism, though, proved to be a controversial practice, as some observers were disturbed by mesmerist claims of mental penetration. "In some cases, in which a female subject seemingly fell sway to a male mesmerist's control, the situation resonated with erotic tension," historian Barbara Weisberg noted. (91) The erotic tension experienced during Mesmerism became apparent to contemporary observers. Writing to his fiancée, the writer Nathaniel Hawthorne admonished Sophia Peabody to avoid mesmerism at all costs, proclaiming that the "sacredness of an individual is violated by it." Hawthorne further asserted that "there would be an intrusion into thy holy of holies," and more horrifying, "the intruder would not be thy husband!" (92)

Abraham Lincoln did not share Hawthorne's fears that Mary's "holy of holies" was going to be violated and allowed Alfred Bledsoe, a fellow border at the Globe Tavern, to mesmerize his wife. (93) Rather than being horrified by the proceedings, Abraham was intrigued by his wife's mesmerism. "Mr. Lincoln was profoundly interested in these experiments," a witness remembered. (94) Though he was an enthusiastic bystander to his wife's Mesmerism, Abraham remained unconvinced of the validity of the practice.

Unfortunately, Mesmerism did not cure Mary's migraines and the couple did not become devotees of Anton Mesmer. Instead, the Lincolns devoted their time and energy on Abraham Lincoln's growing political career and raising their two sons—Robert Todd and Edward "Eddie" Baker. (95) Though Abraham and Mary Lincoln did not embrace Mesmerism, they continued to embrace other metaphysical beliefs.

Lincoln frequently remarked about his belief in the prophetic nature of dreams. While in Washington, D.C. serving in the House of Representatives in 1848, a relieved Abraham Lincoln wrote to Mary. "I did not get rid of the impression of that foolish dream about dear Bobby till I got your letter written the same day," Lincoln admitted. (96) To some of his associates, Lincoln's dreams and visions came from a medical issue, rather than from the other side. Lincoln's first law partner, John T. Stuart, declared that Lincoln's liver "failed to work properly—did not secrete bile—and his bowels were equally as inactive," which caused his vivid dreams. (97) Despite some of his associate's skepticism regarding the prophecy of dreams and visions, Lincoln continued to believe in his dreams for the remainder of his life.

Along with relying on the prophecy of dreams, Abraham Lincoln is also believed to have placed great faith in the power of mad stones to draw out the venom from a snake bite or to cure rabies. (98) Legend holds that Abraham and Mary Lincoln took their son Robert to Terre Haute, Indiana after the young boy was bitten by a dog. Fearful that he might have contracted rabies, the Lincolns' took Robert to Indiana to touch a mad stone. (99) If this story is true, this incident illustrates the Lincolns' willingness to try metaphysical practices to protect their children from harm.

Abraham and Mary Lincoln showered love and affection on their young sons. Yet neither the love nor prayers of a parent or the power of a mad stone could prevent the death of one of their children. Like countless 19th-century parents, the Lincolns suffered the devastating loss of their three-year-old son, Eddie, on February 1, 1850 from pulmonary tuberculosis. (100) The death of their child proved devastating for Abraham and Mary Lincoln. After Eddie's death, Mary was inconsolable, consumed by grief she experienced periods of uncontrollable weeping accompanied by a lack of appetite. (101) This behavior concerned her husband, who became concerned. In an attempt to rouse her, Abraham went to his wife's bedside and pleaded, "Eat, Mary, for we must live." (102)

Abraham Lincoln was also suffering, but unlike his wife, he "resolved to keep his feelings under a firm sway," a family friend later remembered. (103) The Episcopal faith provided little comfort for the

35

grieving mother. Shortly after Eddie's death, Mary Lincoln returned to the faith of her childhood by joining Springfield's First Presbyterian Church. (104) The move back to her parents' faith stemmed from the sermon preached by First Presbyterian's charismatic Revered James Smith who came into the Lincolns life when he conducted Eddie's funeral service. (105)

James Smith aligned himself with the Old Light Presbyterian doctrine which emphasized God's will and the eventual resurrection of the dead. This emotional religion appealed to Mary Lincoln's emotional personality. (106) Turning to Christianity to soothe their grief, the Lincolns ordered "Of Such Is the Kingdom of Heaven" (107) to be engraved on Eddie's headstone. (108) Following Eddie's death, the Lincolns' religious life changed irrevocably, yet they still held onto their metaphysical beliefs.

After her husband's death, Mary declared, "From the time of the death of our little Edward, I believe my husband's heart, was directed towards religion & as time passed on—when Mr. Lincoln became elevated to Office—with the care of a great Nation upon his shoulders—when devastating war was upon us—then indeed to my knowledge—did his great heart go up daily, hourly, in prayer to God—for his sustaining power." (109)

During this period, Spiritualism officially arrived in Springfield. Since 1849, the Whig controlled newspaper, the *Daily Illinois State Journal*, had been following the emergence of Spiritualism with unmitigated contempt. By 1851, the editors sadly realized that Spiritualism was not going to disappear any time soon and concluded, "We shall not be surprised if our city is soon visited by some of the dealers in this spiritual humbuggery (sic)." (110)

Despite these dire predictions, Spiritualism did not make its public appearance in Springfield until 1858 when Leo Miller arrived in town and delivered his anti-Spiritualist lecture at Concert Hall. "He promises a clear explanation of his experiments, which have been given the last two evenings, and which have excited so much curiosity; and we can assure all that it will be made, much to the surprise, interest…his numerous hearers," enthused the editor of the *Daily Illinois State Journal* on March 3, 1858. (111) While it impossible to know if either of the Lincolns' attended any of Leo Miller's lectures it is likely that they were aware of the excitement surrounding Miller's appearance in town.

Though Spiritualism may have taken some time to arrive in Springfield, the town's residents had been well informed about the progression of Spiritualist belief from reading the *Daily Illinois State Journal* and the *Daily Illinois State Register* which avidly followed the religion's development. Leo Miller's anti-Spiritualist lecture would be only the beginning of the Spiritualist wave that would engulf Springfield in 1858.

On October 20, 1858, the *Daily Illinois State Journal* informed readers, "Persons desirous of learning something in regard to the doctrines of Spiritualism will have an opportunity of listening to a course of lectures through the organism of Miss M.F. Hulett, a young lady of seventeen years of age." Though normally taking a skeptical view of Spiritualism, the newspaper concluded, "Miss Hulett is a trance, or inspirational medium, and is said to possess remarkable gifts of eloquence and reasoning." (112)

Following on the heels of Miss Hulett, R.P. Ambler arrived in Springfield where he offered the residents a two-night lecture on "Spiritualism in its Relations to Christianity" on November 17-18, 1858. (113) The year ended with the Spiritualist lecture series conducted by Emma Hardinge in December. Hardinge regaled Springfield with three lectures entitled, "The Spiritualism of the Past," "The Spiritualism of the Present," and "Spiritualism of the Future." (114) Hardinge would eventually gain fame as one of the first chroniclers of Spiritualism's history.

Emma Hardinge would not be the only famous Spiritualist lecturer to come to Springfield. In December 1859, Achsa W. Sprague graced

Springfield with her presence. Sprague thrilled audiences with her recitation of how the spirits had healed her so that she could become the conduit for the spirits. (115) By this time the editor of the *Daily Illinois State Journal* was tired with the glut of Spiritualists lectures that had made a stop in Springfield. "Her lecture last evening was well attended. She spoke under alleged spiritual influence. Her manner of speaking was unexceptionable; and so were her ideas—many of which were probably new to most of her audience," the newspaper declared in its review of Sprague's lecture. (116)

Evidence exists that the Lincolns' did attend séances in Springfield during this period. Writing to the Spiritualist magazine the *Religio-Philosophical Journal* William H. Herndon declared in 1885, "I know nothing of Lincoln's belief or disbelief in Spiritualism." Continuing his letter to the editor in response to an article written by Cyrus Oliver Poole about the President's religious beliefs Herndon asserted, "I cannot say that he believed in Spiritualism, nor can I say that he did not believe in it. He made no revelations to me on this subject, but I have grounds outside, or besides, Mr. Poole's evidences, of the probability of the fact that he did sometimes attend here, in this city [Springfield], séances. I am told this by Mr. Ordway, a Spiritualist. I know nothing of this fact on my personal knowledge." (117)

William H. Herndon's account in 1885 may not have been entirely accurate. While he might have been uncertain about his law partner's opinion about Spiritualism, Abraham Lincoln was exposed to Spiritualist doctrine within his own law office. In July 1867, Lincoln's junior law partner, William H. Herndon, gave a reporter a tour of the late president's law office. The tour concluded with an examination of the office's bookshelf which contained the law books of Abraham Lincoln. "In the southwest corner are more law-books, and at the back of the room near the door stands an old book-case...whose shelves illustrate a very eccentric range beyond the 'stern mistress' of the profession," the reporter noted. (118)

Intermixed between volumes on law and grammar were two volumes on Spiritualism. On the first shelf was Robert Dale Owen's, *Footfalls on the Boundary of another World* and on the second shelf was Andrew Jackson Davis, *The Great Harmonia: Being a Philosophical Revelation of the Natural, Spiritual, and Celestial Universe*. (119) Both works were popular Spiritualists tracts which elaborated on the central tenets of Spiritualism. While it is unclear on whether the two volumes on Spiritualism belonged to Abraham Lincoln or William Herndon, it is significant that Lincoln was exposed to Spiritualist belief within his own law office.

During the tour of the law office given in 1867, Herndon intimated that most of the books in the law office had belonged to Abraham Lincoln. "There, are the law books of our firm. I am about to withdraw from practice. Were I disposed I could sell those books for a price, but I shall let Robert Lincoln take them," Herndon declared to the reporter. (120) Though Herndon does not mention who owned the other books, Mary Lincoln considered the books in her husband's law office to have been her husband's property. In 1874, Mary Lincoln complained to her cousin John Todd Stuart that Herndon had stolen "my husband's law books & our own private library, *we* may *safely* call him thief." (121)

Following Lincoln's death, Dr. J. Ridgeley Martin signed an affidavit that, "he was a close neighbor for a period of three years in Springfield, Illinois, studied law in a building where he had his office…and the medium's name [was] Thorp… Mr. Lincoln received messages from his mother and Ann Rutledge." (122) Though Martin may have been influenced by the rumors of Lincoln's love affair with Ann Rutledge in the 1830's, it is still interesting to note that there was a Spiritualist medium practicing in one of the buildings that housed Lincoln's law office. Besides encountering Spiritualism at the law office, Abraham and Mary Lincoln knew and socialized with Spiritualists while they resided in Springfield. (123)

41

Chapter Four

"It is hard, hard to have him die!"

November 6, 1860 had been a long and exhausting day for Abraham and Mary Lincoln. After spending the night with her husband awaiting the election returns at the Illinois Statehouse and at a local restaurant where dinner had been prepared for the election party Mary Lincoln had returned home. (124) Finally at around 11:30 p.m., Mary decided to give up her vigil and went to bed. (125) Across town at the restaurant, Abraham Lincoln was also waiting for the election results.

Around 1:00 A.M, Abraham received the good news that the Republican Party had carried New York. (126) After years of political setbacks, all of Abraham and Mary Lincoln's shared ambitions had finally paid off—Abraham Lincoln had been elected the sixteenth president of the United States. President-elect Lincoln was ecstatic declaring to his aides, "I guess there's a little lady at home who would like to hear this news." (127) Rushing home, Lincoln found his wife sound asleep in their bed. Rousing his wife, Lincoln exclaimed, "Mary, Mary, *we* are elected." (128)

During the election night excitement, President-elect Abraham Lincoln would have a vision that would remain with him for the rest of his life. Following the 1864 election, President Lincoln recounted the vision he witnessed to his friend Noah Brooks. (129) According to Lincoln, he had just reclined on a lounge in his bedroom when he spied an unusual reflection in a bureau mirror.

"Looking in that glass, I saw myself reflected, nearly at full length; but my face, I noticed, had *two* separate and distinct images, the tip of the nose of one being about three inches from the tip of the other. I was a little bothered, perhaps startled, and got up and looked in the glass, but the illusion vanished," the President recounted. (130) Upon returning to the lounge, he noticed the image again and this time the vision was more vivid.

"On lying down again I saw it a second time—plainer, if possible, than before; and then I noticed that one of the faces was a little paler, say five shades, than the other. I got up and the thing melted away, and I went off and, in the excitement of the hour, forgot all about it—nearly, but not quite, for the thing would once in a while come up, and give me a little pang, as though something uncomfortable had happened," Lincoln informed Brooks. (131)

Still bothered by the image in the mirror, Lincoln turned to Mary for her opinion on the meaning of the vision. Upset by what her husband had seen in his mirror, Mary interpreted the vision to be a dire warning. "She thought it was 'a sign' that I was to be elected to a second term of office, and that the paleness of one of the faces was an omen that I should not see life through the last term," the President concluded. (132)

Clearly this vision held some meaning for Abraham Lincoln. Though Noah Brooks tried to assert that the vision held no meaning for the President, claiming in July 1865, "The President, with his usual good sense, saw nothing in all this but an optical illusion; though the flavor of superstition which hangs about every man's composition made him wish that he had never seen it." (133)

Whatever Lincoln saw and whatever he might have thought about the vision, the image in his mirror on election night stayed with him for the remainder of his life. Despite some of his associate's skepticism for dreams and omens serving as harbingers of the future, President Lincoln continued to rely on his dreams after being elected. "In the old days God and His angels came to men in their sleep and made themselves known through dreams. Nowadays dreams are regarded as very foolish and are seldom told, except by old women and young men and maidens in love," Lincoln declared. (134)

The President-elect had a good reason to feel uneasy about his future presidency. His election as the first Republican president divided the nation over slavery sparking the Civil War. While President Lincoln received enough Electoral College votes to win the election, he did not receive the majority in the popular vote. (135) In many Southern states, Abraham Lincoln's name was not even listed on the ballots. In this climate of hostility, many Americans—in the North and the South—carried a negative view of the President-elect and his wife. While many Americans were unsure about Abraham and Mary Lincoln, back in Springfield, the Lincolns were receiving the congratulations of their friends and neighbors.

During this period, Mary Lincoln sorted through the family's possessions, determining which items would come with the family to Washington. (136) For an unknown reason several personal letters were either deemed unimportant or were seen by Mary as too personal and were destroyed in a bonfire in the alley behind the Lincolns home. (137) As Mary Lincoln was sorting through her possessions in perpetration for the family's move to Washington, D.C., the President-elect also began to prepare for the challenges that faced him as the nation began to split apart at the seams.

Concerned Americans from both the North and South flooded his mailbox with letters expressing their advice, warnings, and in some cases threats toward Lincoln and his family. (138) "God damn your god damned old Hellfired god damned soul to hell god damn you and god dam your god damned family's god damned hellfired god damned soul to hell," Pete Muggins raved in a letter to "Old Abe Lincoln." (139) Spiritualists, understanding the dire threat that Lincoln was facing from Southern secessionists, began to conduct séances in an attempt to get advice from the other side on how to save the country from war.

Feeling that they offered an answer, a few Spiritualists wrote and visited the President-elect with their suggestions and warnings. Shortly after the election, President-elect Lincoln was visited by the Chicago Spiritualist Thomas Richmond. A committed Spiritualist, Richmond felt compelled to visit the future president at his election headquarters to warn the President-elect that he would be assassinated.

According to Thomas Richmond, Lincoln asked him why he believed that harm would befall him. "I said that the South was not satisfied with his election; and in the two instances before, that they were dissatisfied—Harrison and Taylor, were both poisoned soon after taking their seats. I advised him to be careful who he had about him, and who prepared his food," Richmond recalled in his memoir. (140)

Unswayed by Richmond's warning President-elect Lincoln politely dismissed the Spiritualist declaring, "If they are determined to assassinate me, they will do it." (141) Despite his apathy towards Richmond warning, the President-elect continued to receive letters written by the faithful with dire warnings about the threats that he faced in the nation's capital.

In December 1860, President-elect Abraham Lincoln received a letter from a devoted Republican who called himself "G.A. A Wide Awake." G. A. began his missive by reinforcing his loyalty to the President-elect's declaring, "I am a good Republican." To strengthen his cause, G.A. even signed his name "A Wide Awake," and it is likely that the young man belonged to the Wide Awake Clubs organized by the Republican Party for the 1860 election. (142)

After reassuring the President-elect that he was a Republican Party loyalist, G.A. had some distressing news to relate. "I deem it my duty, to communicate the following facts: In the dwelling in which I reside, a Young Girl lives, who is a singular rare phenomena. She is a Sonalmbulist, a Clairvoyant (not a Spiritualist), in a very highly developed State. Last evening she requested my presence, I found her in a trance. She communicated to me the following circumstances and requested me, to warn Your Excellency," G.A. intoned. (143)

The young man forwarded the clairvoyant's message warning President-elect Lincoln of an assassination plot to poison him upon his arrival in Washington, D.C. The mysterious and cryptic G.A. concluded his letter by declaring that "The undersigned is no Spiritualist, but is free from any similar prejudice; but knows the absolute verity of many events foretold by this Sonambule,—and therefore in the interest of Your Excellency, of this country and of the Republican party, implores Your Excellency, not to disregard this Admonition." (144) G.A.'s denial over being a Spiritualist highlighted the negative reaction Spiritualism aroused in many Americans.

Even if G.A. was telling the truth, his letter to President-elect Lincoln testified to how far Spiritualism had permeated American culture on the eve of the Civil War. As historian Drew Gilpin Faust noted, "By the time war broke out, spiritualist notions were sufficiently common to influence and engage even those who were not formal adherents." (145) Clearly G.A. sincerely believed in the young medium and was so alarmed by her prediction that he felt compelled to warn the President-elect. Despite the warnings, the Lincolns' departed for Washington, D.C.

The Lincoln family traveled in high style to the nation's capital in a specially appointed train car. Along the route to Washington, the Lincolns where warmly welcomed. While Democrats were dissatisfied with the outcome of the presidential election, Republicans were elated that their party had won. "I want to live more than I have done for years; to see the future of this great nation under its new impulse of regeneration," one party loyalist crowed. (146)

Spiritualists also had cause to rejoice due to a rumor circling that President-elect Lincoln was one of them. On March 12, 1861, the Wisconsin *Waukesha Freeman,* which according to its masthead was "A Weekly Newspaper—Devoted to Republican Politics, Literature, and the News of the day," published the starting details under the headline, "The President Elect a Spiritualist." (147) The article published the account of the trance medium J.B. Conklin. According to the revelations of Conklin, Abraham Lincoln, before his presidential nomination, had attended at least two spirit circles conducted by him.

According to the article, J.B. Conklin discovered the identity of his mysterious customer after he saw the President-elect during his journey to Washington, D.C. "Being a Republican himself and not wishing to run an opposition to the distinguished visitant, he [Conklin] broke up his own Levees at the 'Jackson' [Hotel] to attend that of the 'Weddell' [Hotel]. The moment he sat eyes on the Lion of the occasion he recognized in him a very peculiar individual he had met at his rooms in New York, but at the time did not know his name," the article proclaimed. (148)

Surprisingly, the author of the article saw no problem in the President-elect's belief in Spiritualism. The lack of criticism about Lincoln's association with Spiritualists would continue within Republican publications throughout the Civil War. The author concluded, "So with this link of connection established between the spheres, spiritual association with the patriots of the past, thus availing himself of the wisdom of the two worlds; the President elect ought to have his political pathway so enlightened as to give the country assurances of perpetual union and peace." (149) Despite the hopeful tone of this article, many still doubted that President-elect Lincoln could handle the coming storm.

Not even the glamour of the Inaugural Ball could ward off the social chill that surrounded the Lincolns' in Washington, D.C. On the eve of war, Washington's Southern residents were skeptical about Abraham and Mary Lincoln's western manners and Republican politics. Many Northerners doubted that President Lincoln possessed the strength or judgment to be president. This opinion is illustrated in a horoscope published about President Lincoln. In an installment of *Broughton's Monthly Planet Reader and Astrological Journal*, the self proclaimed Dr.

L.D. Broughton asserted that President Lincoln's horoscope made him unfit to lead the nation.

Writing in the May-June 1861 issue, Broughton asserted that President Lincoln, "had very unfortunate aspects in his Nativity at the time he was elected, he had Mars over the Sun's place in opposition to Jupiter, besides several other very evil aspects, which makes us judge that it will be one of the worst things that could have happened to the United States, Abram Lincoln being elected President. The evil will not be felt in its force right away. We look for something particular happening ABOUT NEXT APRIL or MAY, 1861." (150) It appeared that the war Dr. Broughton's prediction of discord proved correct, after months of saber rattling, war officially began on April 12, 1861 when the Southern militia opened fire on Fort Sumter located in Charleston, South Carolina.

Further darkening the North's spirits, the summer of 1861 witnessed an appearance of a comet that many viewed as a portent of dark days ahead for the nation. (151) Julia Taft remembered the stir the comet's appearance caused in her Washington, D.C. neighborhood. Years later in her memoir, Julia recalled the prediction made by the slave Oola who was known as a conjurer. "You see dat great fire sword, blazin' in de sky," Oola said in reference to the comet. "Dat's a great war comin' and de handle's to'rd de Norf and de point to'rd de Souf and de Norf's gwine take dat sword and cut de Souf's heart out. But dat Linkum man, chilluns, if he takes de sword, he's gwine perish by it," Oola told Julia. (152)

Julia Taft's brother's were intrigued by Oola's prophecy and quickly informed their friends Tad and Willie Lincoln. Though not wanting to alarm their friends, the children left out Oola's dire warning about the President. "Tad was greatly impressed and carried the story, as tidings of import, to his father. Mrs. Lincoln laughed, but the President seemed strangely interested," Julia recalled. (153) President Lincoln appeared to be deeply affected by Oola's prophecy. "I noticed him, a few evenings later, looking out of the window intently at the comet and I wondered if he was thinking of the old Negro woman's prophecy," Julia Taft reflected in her memoir. (154) The comet would not be the only warning the President received.

The flood of letters that had started in Springfield, Illinois continued after Lincolns' change of address. Among the dozens of letters he received on a daily basis, the President still continued to receive letters from Spiritualists. Despite receiving letters from Spiritualists, President Lincoln, at this time, possessed little interest in the faith. After listening to celebrated author Robert Dale Owen's discourse on Spiritualism in

1861, the President is said to have quipped, "Well, for those who like that sort of thing I should think that is just about the sort of thing they would like." (155)

For President Lincoln, "that sort of thing" did not appeal to him yet. Undeterred by the President's lack of interest in the movement, Spiritualists continued to write to the President with advice and warnings from the spirit world. One such correspondent was a gentleman by the name of J.S. Hastings who wrote to President Lincoln frequently during the Civil War. "I have been for three years an undoubting believer in Spirit Communion—I have a numerous family of Children, Wives, Brothers & Sisters, and many friends in Spirit life, with whom I have directly or indirectly in almost daily communion—Therefore Spirit Communion is as much a truth with me, as the events of my daily life—so much I deem proper to justify the communication referred to," Hastings testified to Lincoln on August 9, 1861. (156)

After this lengthy introduction, Hastings informed the President that while attending a Spiritualist séance the medium in charge "was controuled by one purporting to be my son—in life a Presbyterian Clergyman, and whose identity I did not doubt—He told me that I had been brought there from my known faith in the truth of Spirit Communion, and my fearlessness in acting under its influence—He also said that the traitors about you were under the influence of demons—once in the form, and that their power for evil was past comprehension—that all the higher spirits could do was to give you timely warning—." (157)

The President was as likely as unimpressed by this letter as he was with G.A.'s warnings from December 1860, as there was no evidence that the President responded to Hastings' letter. President Lincoln continued to receive more letters from the undefeatable J.H. Hastings. In his second letter to the President, Hastings had a dual purpose in writing. While his first letter warned of demons that were influencing the course of events that were prolonging the Civil War, in the second letter the gentleman changed tactics.

The first course of action J.S. Hastings wished to discuss with President Lincoln was his plan for emancipation. Under Hastings' plan, Southern slaves would pay the state and local governments for their freedom. (158) After dispensing with his plan regarding the gradual emancipation of Southern slaves that would bring a peaceful end to both the war and the issue of slavery, Hastings moved on to the heart of his letter to the President. Once again, Hastings wanted to relay to President Lincoln the results of a Spiritualist séance he had attended.

During the previous séance attended by J.S. Hastings, the medium claimed he had channeled with Hastings' deceased son. The second time around the medium claimed that he had contacted the much more prestigious spirits of John C. Calhoun and Daniel Webster who informed the medium and Hastings that they had a message for President Lincoln. (159) The fact that J.S. Hastings continued to write to President Lincoln despite the lack of evidence that the President even responded to his letters highlighted the deep conviction Spiritualist possessed regarding their faith and the validity of Spiritualism.

The letters that Hastings continued to write to President Lincoln proved that he genuinely believed that the messages he received from Spiritualist mediums could help the Union win the Civil War. As 1861 gradually drew to a close, J.S. Hastings was not the only Spiritualist who wrote to the President.

As the carnage of the Civil War gradually became apparent to the Northern populace who had initially expected the war to be relative short and bloodless, President Lincoln began to receive letters from the dead. By December 1861, President Lincoln had already lost two close friends, Elmer Ellsworth and Edward D. Baker on the field of battle. (160) Edward D. Baker's death must have been particularly difficult for the Lincolns' as they had named their son Eddie after their friend. (161)

Now both Edward's were gone. Not long after Baker's death, the President received a letter from the Spiritualist medium J.B. Conklin, the same medium who had claimed to have met President Lincoln at a sé-ance, which contained a purported message from Baker. "My esteemed and best earthly friends," Edward D. Baker proclaimed through Conklin. After this greeting, Baker affirmed his continued loyalty to the Union. (162) Then Baker offered President Lincoln a description of what it is like on the other side. "I am not dead. I still live, a conscious individual, with hope, aspirations and interest; for the Union still alive. I experi-enced a happy reality—a glorious change, by the process termed 'death,'" Baker proclaimed through the medium. (163) "I would like to communicate with you personally, if not now, after the close of your offi-cial term. I will be with you in spirit, and with many others impress and strengthen you," Baker proclaimed.

Hinting that there was more that Baker wanted to tell his friend, the spirit abruptly concluded his letter writing, "Man lives on Earth, to live elsewhere, and that elsewhere is ever present. Heaven and Hell are conditions, not localities." (164) Sadly, Edward D. Baker would not be the last close friend or family member that President Lincoln would lose during the Civil War.

The Washington, D.C. newspapers were full of obituaries. The Civil War was claiming the lives of countless soldiers in the camps and hospitals. The nation's capital had become increasingly over crowded since the start of the Civil War. The extra soldiers needed to provide for the city's defense had swelled the population of Washington, D.C. to a critical level. This concerned the city's residents, as the *Washington Evening Star* asked, "Are we to have pestilence among us?" (165)

This dramatic influx to the population overtaxed Washington's primitive sewer system which endangered the health of the civilian population. On February 21, 1862 the *Washington Evening Star* reported on the death of another victim of the war. He was not a general or even a common soldier, but the 11-year-old son of President Lincoln. Willie Lincoln had been ill for several days with typhoid fever contracted from drinking water tainted from the waste of the camps stationed along the Potomac River. (166) After suffering for several days, the *Washington Evening Star* reported, "he lingered until 5 o'clock in the afternoon, when his spirit was released." (167)

For the second time Abraham and Mary Lincoln had lost a beloved son. Willie Lincoln's death emotionally and physically devastated his mother who was already exhausted from the strain of nursing Willie and her youngest son Tad who had also contracted typhoid fever. If Mary Lincoln expected her own romanticized version of the Christian Good Death, she was sadly disappointed. The Christian Good Death had become enshrined in American culture by the time of the Civil War.

Death took place at home with the immediate family clustered around the dying person where they would analyze the last moments to insure that the family would be reunited in heaven. (168)

Rather than enacting his own version of the Christian Good Death, Willie had slipped into a coma before he died, depriving his mother of any final words that she could look back on for solace. (169) Instead, the boy died quietly with his parents at his bedside. Mary summoned her seamstress and friend Elizabeth Keckly to the White House where she washed and laid out Willie's body for burial. While Elizabeth was preparing Willie's body, President Lincoln entered his son's bedroom, "He came to the bed, lifted the cover from the face of his child, gazed at it long and earnestly murmuring, 'My poor boy, he was too good for this earth'," Elizabeth remembered. (170) "God has called him home. I know that he is much better off in heaven, but we loved him so. It is hard, hard to have him die!" Abraham cried. (171) Indeed, Willie's death proved more than the Lincolns' could fathom. In an attempt to sooth their grief Abraham and Mary Lincoln would turn to their metaphysical beliefs.

Part Two

"Mr. Lincoln Must Hear What We Have Heard"

On a cold December night in 1862, an unlikely group arrived at the White House. They had been expected and were ushered into the Red Parlor. (172) Since Willie's death earlier in the year, Abraham and Mary Lincoln had canceled the lavish public entertainments that had marked their first year in the Presidential Mansion. (173) Instead, in their grief, the couple preferred quiet evenings at home spent in the company of close friends. On this particular evening the invited guests were a contingent of Spiritualists lead by the 21-year-old medium, Nettie Colburn. They had been invited by Mary Lincoln to conduct a séance in the White House.

The year 1862 had been a particularly bad year for the Lincolns. Beside the loss of their beloved son Willie, the Civil War had been going badly for the Union. Further adding to President Lincoln's woes, the Union had just suffered another devastating defeat at the Battle of Fredericksburg, Virginia. (174) In an attempt to provide comfort for her beleaguered husband, Mary Lincoln invited Nettie Colburn to introduce her husband to Spiritualism.

Chapter Five

"My heart yearns to see her seeking comfort besides these unstable pleasures"

Mary Lincoln was consumed with grief following Willie's death on February 21, 1862. The grieving mother remained bedridden with Elizabeth Keckly as her only attendant. Down the hall, Tad lay critically ill with the same illness that had killed his brother. (175) Mary Lincoln's wild expressions of grief concerned her husband, who came into his wife's bedroom and according to Elizabeth Keckley, gently pulled Mary from her bed and took her to the window, "with a stately solemn gesture he pointed to the lunatic asylum," Elizabeth remembered.

Addressing his wife, President Lincoln asked, "Mother, do you see that white building on the hill yonder?" "Try and control your grief, or it will drive you mad, and we will have to send you there," Abraham warned. (176) Her husband's warning shocked Mary out of her stupor, just as his plea 12 years earlier to eat had brought her back to reality following Eddie's death. (177)

Like she had done a decade before, Mary Lincoln rallied herself for the sake of her remaining family members. Though this time, returning to a sense of normalcy proved to be more difficult as the First Lady struggled to cope with the death of her beloved Willie. The loss of her child threw Mary into a deep depression. Following Willie's death, Mary refused to enter the boy's bedroom and the Green Room where his funeral had been held. (178)

"There was something supernatural in her dread of these things, and something that she could not explain," Elizabeth Keckly commented in her memoir. (179) Fortunately for the Lincolns', by the end of February Tad's health began to improve. The news of his improvement spread across the North. On February 27, 1862 the *Chicago Daily Tribune* reported that "Mrs. Lincoln and her youngest son, who have been very ill, are improving." (180)

Sometime during 1862, Mary Lincoln turned to Spiritualism. Like many aspects regarding the metaphysical life of the Lincolns', it is unclear who introduced Mary Lincoln to Washington D.C.'s Spiritualist community. For decades biographers, such as Jean Baker and Elizabeth Fleischner have argued that it was Elizabeth Keckly who introduced Mary Lincoln to Spiritualism. (181) Yet, there is no concrete evidence to support this claim. The only link that connected Elizabeth Keckly to Spiritualism was in the memoir of Noah Brooks. Brooks connected Elizabeth Keckly as the person who introduced Mary Lincoln to a Spiritualist medium in his post-war memoir of life in the capital. (182) From this one sentence in Brooks' memoir, historians have taken it as proof that Elizabeth Keckly was the person that introduced Mary Lincoln to Spiritualism in 1862.

Born a slave in Virginia, Elizabeth Keckly would have been introduced to the metaphysical beliefs of her fellow slaves. (183) Yet there is no evidence that Elizabeth Keckly was involved in the capitals Spiritualist community. Besides Elizabeth Keckly, historians have offered other candidates. Jason Emerson has suggested that Mary Lincoln was introduced to Spiritualism by her friend, Dr. Anson G. Henry, based on an 1865 letter the doctor wrote to his wife where he took credit for the First Lady's conversion to Spiritualism. (184)

Elizabeth Keckly was not the only person caring for Mary Lincoln in the days following Willie's death. Mary Jane Welles, the wife of Gideon Welles, had formed a friendship with the First Lady. Following Willie's death Mary Jane Welles came to the White House to assist the Lincoln family. (185) Mary Jane was also a committed Spiritualist who began attending séances with her husband following the death of their daughter in 1854. (186) It is possible that during these dark days Mary Jane Welles shared her belief in Spiritualism with Mary Lincoln which sparked an interest in the grieving mother.

Long before Willie's death, Mary Lincoln already had a well-known interest in metaphysical beliefs. "It was said that Mrs. Lincoln believed in signs but the President believed in dreams," Julia Taft Bayne remembered in her memoir. (187) This openness to metaphysical beliefs would play a crucial role in her introduction to Spiritualism. Mary Lincoln's involvement in Spiritualism would prove to be a controversial move. Though the religion was flourishing, it still remained unpopular in conservative circles.

For whatever reason, Mary Lincoln found Spiritualism to be an appealing doctrine. The death of Willie proved to be unbearable for his mother. Mary struggled to understand why God had taken away such a promising, bright boy. "Willie, she often said, if spared by Providence, would be the hope and stay of her old age," Elizabeth Keckly later remembered. (188) For Mary Lincoln, accepting Willie's death as part of God's plan was simply impossible.

Beginning in 1862, Mary Lincoln began visiting Spiritualists in Washington, D.C. in an attempt to contact Willie's spirit. The devastation wrought by the Civil War had turned 1862 into a good year for Spiritualist mediums. In the January 11, 1862 issue of the Spiritualist newspaper *The Herald of Progress* featured ads for four medical clairvoyants,

12 public mediums, and notices that four Spiritualist associations were holding meetings open to the public. (189)

Satisfied with what she saw and heard during these séances, Mary Lincoln developed an ardent interest in Spiritualism. What she witnessed during the spirit circles provided proof for the First Lady that she was in contact with the spirits of her deceased sons. This provided a powerful comfort for the grieving mother. Through the spirit raps and trance messages relayed by mediums, Mary became convinced that she was speaking to the spirits of Willie and Eddie. For Mary Lincoln this provided undisputable proof that heaven existed and that her children were there waiting for the day when the family would be re-united.

Fortunately Washington, D.C. already had a flourishing Spiritualist community since the 1850's. According to Spiritualist chronicler E.W. Capron who published his study on Spiritualism in 1855, "Conferences are held weekly, at which the public have the opportunity to hear and discuss the subjects involved in [Spiritual] philosophy." (190) Though the city proved receptive towards Spiritualism, some mediums found Washingtonians to be rude during séances. In a letter to a friend, Kate Fox complained about the behavior of her clients who arrived drunk and addressed her with "mean, low remarks." (191) To preserve her privacy and the dignity of her position, Mary Lincoln attended private séances. While Mary may have converted to Spiritualism, not all of her acquaintances approved of her new faith.

During her period of sorrow, Mary Lincoln turned to Rebecca Pomroy, who had served as a nurse in the White House during Tad's illness. Both women had suffered the devastating loss of a child that had tested their faith. The main difference that separated Rebecca Pomroy and Mary Lincoln was the manner in which they dealt with their grief. While Rebecca developed a deep evangelical faith that helped her accept her losses, Mary turned to Spiritualism. (192) Mary Lincoln shared with Pomroy her belief in Spiritualism—a belief that the nurse did not share. Despite Rebecca Pomroy's disapproval of Mary's interest in Spiritualism, this did not dissuade the willful First Lady from trying to convert her friend.

Since Mary Lincoln failed to convince Rebecca Pomroy of the veracity of Spiritualism in person she turned to an intermediary to speak with her friend. While on duty at the military hospital at Columbia College in April 1862, Rebecca received an unexpected visitor. Reverend John Pierpont, a Boston Spiritualist and friend of the First Lady, arrived bearing a letter of introduction from Mary. Pierpont announced to Rebecca that the purpose of his visit was to convey to her an important letter from a spirit medium that contained a message from her departed son. Shocked, Rebecca Pomroy opened the letter,

"Found it purporting to come from my Willie to his mother, in which he says that 'he is happy, and wants her to
feel him as always around her; but she heeds him not, and
when she is tired in heart, closing the eyes of those dear
ones committed to her care, he wishes to commune with
her, and try to ease her mind and make her happy. He has
formed the acquaintance of Willie Lincoln in the spirit
world, and when his mother was at the White House, the
two spirits came and hovered over Willie Lincoln's mother, so that she felt them near, while his mother will take no
heed to the spirit influence of her dear son. She often
looks at his lock of hair and weeps like a child that will
not be comforted.'" (193)

Instead of convincing Rebecca Pomroy that the message had come from her son, the nurse was dismayed. Pomroy tried to show Revered Pierpont the error of his ways, arguing that the message had come from a Spiritualist medium that had been an acquaintance of her late husband and as a result the medium was already privy to this infor-mation and had used it in composing the letter. Despite her argument,

John Pierpont remained as committed to his beliefs as Rebecca Pomroy was to hers.

"But of course this theory would not satisfy Mr. Pierpont, and he went away disappointed that he could not make a Spiritualist of me," Rebecca concluded in a letter to a friend. (194) Undismayed by her failure to convert her friend, Mary Lincoln remained committed to her belief in Spiritualism and continued to share her beliefs with Rebecca Pomroy.

Mary Lincoln, in her grief, turned to Rebecca as an outlet for her grief and the two frequently discussed their personal faith. "We have frequent conversations on these things, and my heart yearns to see her seeking comfort in something besides these unstable pleasures," Rebecca declared in a letter in April 1862. (195) Rebecca Pomroy was clearly distressed that Mary Lincoln had turned to Spiritualism instead of copying her example by turning to Evangelical Christianity.

Through Spiritualism, Mary Lincoln began to feel some religious comfort in a way that her Presbyterian faith had failed to do. As her belief in Spiritualism matured, the First Lady became active member in Washington D.C's Spiritualist community. In the process Mary Lincoln became acquainted with a Spiritualist medium Nettie Colburn whose memoirs would provide insight and revelations on the Lincolns' involvement with Spiritualism during the Civil War.

Chapter Six

"Some new and powerful influence obtained possession of my organism"

The Civil War made Washington, D.C. a Spiritualist Mecca, attracting countless Spiritualist mediums that came to the capital to conduct séances for government officials, members of the Union army, and for the grieving family members who had lost a loved one in the conflict. (196) One such medium was Nettie Colburn, a young trance medium from upstate New York. As a child, Nettie had discovered her talents for mediumship which she had transformed into a successful career as a Spiritualist lecturer. (197)

"It came to me in a sense unsought, and took me, an untaught child, from my humble home in the ranks of the laboring people, and led me forth, a teacher of the sublime truth of immortality opening to me the doors of the wealthy and the prominent, as well as leading among the poor and lowly, speaking through my un-conscious lips words of strength and consolation, suited to all conditions, until everywhere, from the father's quiet fireside to the palatial city mansion, I found only words of welcome and kindly care," Nettie Colburn declared in 1891.

By 1862, the petite, 21-year-old had become a successful and popular speaker on the Spiritualist lecture circuit. During one lecture, Nettie went into a trance where the medium claimed that she was informed by her spirit guide that there was a "Congress of spirits" comprised of leading Americans on the other side that had selected her for an important mission. While Nettie never listed the members of the "Congress of spirits," Fayette Hall a critic of Spiritualism and an acquaintance of Nettie during the Civil War declared in his 1902 exposé that the members of the Congress were not as prominent as the medium claimed:

> "She went to President Lincoln from Bolton, Connecticut, by spirit direction, accompanied by her band of spirits, consisting of Romano, who seems to have been more ornamental than useful, Wisdom, who is seldom spoken of as being of much importance, Priscilla, of John Alden fame, who made herself useful in introductory services at the séances, Bright Eyes a little squaw, was known as the medium's familiar spirit, whatever that may have been, Pinkie, an Aztic (sic) Princess, who lived in Mexico five hundred years ago and Dr. Bamford, an old Yankee doctor, who had been her father's family physician in Bolton, where the medium belonged, seems to have been her chief advisement and directing spirits and principals at séances who gave the President important directions." (198)

The spirits that Hall listed in his exposé were spirits that Nettie claimed were her spirit guides. Nowhere in her memoir does she assert that her guides were also members of the Congress of Spirits. Fayette Hall claimed to be a devoted Spiritualist, but during the Civil War he came to believe that President Lincoln had become influenced by demonic entities who communicated through a contingent of Republican Spiritualists. (199)

According to Nettie Colburn, the Congress of Spirits had selected the medium to travel to Washington, D.C. where she would relay their words to President Lincoln. (200) Upon learning what the spirits wanted her to do, Nettie claimed that she was initially incredulous and concluded that she "would find but poor reception in the presence of the first Ruler of the Land." (201) Despite her protests, Nettie Colburn found herself in the nation's capital in December 1862 on family business. (202) While lecturing in Baltimore, Nettie received a letter from her youngest brother stating he was sick in a military hospital and that he needed her help in getting a furlough so that he could recover at home. (203)

Upon her arrival in the capital, Nettie Colburn quickly ingratiated herself within Washington D.C.'s Spiritualist community. The swelling ranks of Washington society brought on by the Civil War included several prominent Spiritualists who quickly welcomed Nettie into their ranks. Thomas Gales Foster, a Spiritualist lecturer and War Department clerk was one such acquaintance.

Through Foster, Nettie became an acquaintance of former Congressman and Spiritualist devotee Daniel E. Somes and the Laurie fami-

70

ly. (204) The Lauries' were successful Spiritualists who hosted séances attended by the city's elite nightly in their Georgetown home. Cranston Laurie, the family's patriarch worked for the Post Office as a mid-level bureaucrat. (205)

By 1854 the family had earned the reputation of "being remarkably under the spiritual influence," Washington, D.C., bureaucrat Benjamin Brown French recorded in his diary. (206) "Mr. and Mrs. Laurie were both fine medium; and I had met many prominent people during my visits there, who, though not professing to be Spiritualists, made no secret of their desire to investigate the subject," Nettie recalled. (207)

At the Laurie house, Nettie Colburn preformed séances in the family's parlor where she met one of the Lauries' clients, First Lady Mary Lincoln. Though the record is silent on how Mary Lincoln became acquainted with the Laurie family, it is likely that the Lincolns met the Laurie family at their church. Cranston Laurie hailed from a prominent Washington family. His father, the Reverend Dr. James Laurie founded the F Street Presbyterian Church, which became the New York Avenue Presbyterian Church. (208) Upon arriving in Washington the Lincolns selected the New York Avenue Presbyterian Church as their place of worship. It is possible that the Lincolns first became acquainted with

Cranston Laurie and his wife while attending the church that the late Dr. Laurie had founded.

During her first meeting with the First Lady, Nettie Colburn wowed Mary with her Spiritualist prowess. Nettie Colburn Maynard later recalled that evening in her memoir, "Some new and powerful influence obtained possession of my organism and addressed Mrs. Lincoln, it seemed, with great clearness and force, upon matters of state." (209) Whatever the medium said during this meeting—and Nettie always claimed that while in a trance she had no memory of what she said—struck a chord with the First Lady. (210) Following the séance, Mary Lincoln was so impressed that she is said to have declared, *"This young lady must not leave Washington. I feel she must stay here, and Mr. Lincoln must hear what we have heard. It is all-important, and he must hear it."* (211) Turning to Nettie, Mary pleaded, "Don't think of leaving Washington, I beg of you. Can you not remain with us?" (212)

Another witness to the séance, Eliza M. Debuy, remembered the events similarly, "In the winter of 1862-1863, I attended a séance at Mrs. Lauries' in Georgetown, where Mrs. Lincoln was present. She was accompanied by Mr. Newton, Commissioner of Agriculture. At the séance, remarkable statements were made, which surprised Mrs. Lincoln to such a degree that she asked that a séance might be given to Mr. Lincoln." (213) To keep Nettie Colburn in the city, Mary Lincoln used her political clout as the President's wife and arranged for her to be employed as a clerk for the Department of Agriculture. (214) Besides assisting Nettie Colburn in finding employment in Washington, Mary Lincoln also assisted Nettie's brother in receiving his furlough, thus began a pattern of mutual benefits for both the medium and the First Lady which would characterize their relationship. (215)

Comforted by Spiritualism Mary Lincoln eagerly shared her new found beliefs with her husband. As she had done with Rebecca Pomroy, Mary Lincoln attempted to convert her husband. While Mary completely failed in her attempt to convert Rebecca Pomroy, it is more difficult to assert that she also failed with her husband. Whatever Mary Lincoln told her husband it kindled an interest to learn more about Spiritualism as Abraham Lincoln was also still grieving Willie's death.

William Carpenter, a painter who lived in the White House for six months in 1864, claimed that following Willie's death the President would lock himself away every Thursday, the day the boy had died. (216) Three months after Willie's death, President Abraham Lincoln expressed his grief by reciting Constance's lament from Shakespeare's *King John* to a group of acquaintances, "That we shall see and know our friends in heaven / If that be true, I shall see my boy again." (217) Turning to an army officer, Lincoln asked, "Did you ever dream of some lost friend, and feel that you were having a sweet communion with him…? That is the way I dream of my lost boy." (218)

On another occasion the President remarked to Salmon P. Chase, Secretary of the Treasury, "Do you ever find yourself talking to the dead? I do…ever since Willie's death. I catch myself involuntarily talking to him as if he were near me…And I feel that he is!" (219) While Mary refused to look at her dead son's possessions, and even banished flowers that were Willie's favorites from the White House, President Lincoln took comfort in hanging a picture painted by Willie in his office. (220) Mary Lincoln saw Spiritualism as the perfect outlet for her husband's grief and as an outlet for the pressures of the Civil War which increased after the President announced that he would sign the Emancipation Proclamation into effect on January 1, 1863.

Viewed today as a landmark decision that changed the Civil War from a battle to preserve the Union to a war over the freedom of the slaves, the Emancipation Proclamation was not greeted with universal acclaim in the North. While President Abraham Lincoln's personal views towards African Americans may have been influenced through his daily contact with the White House's African American servants including Elizabeth Keckly and his contact with the freed people who lived in

74

the contraband camps on the road that led to the Lincolns' summer cottage, the Soldier's Home, many in the North still clung to their prejudices. Northern Democrats were outraged that seemingly overnight the Union's war goals had changed. They were willing to fight a war for the Union—but not one to free the slaves. Abolitionists were also unhappy, while they were relieved that the President was finally moving towards an abolition stance, they were angry that the Emancipation Proclamation only freed the slaves held in Confederate territory and neglected the slaves held in the areas of the South occupied by the Union Army. (221)

While the President expected to receive criticism over the Emancipation Proclamation, the amount he did receive nearly overwhelmed him. (222) The pressure President Lincoln received to retract the Proclamation was intense. As January 1, 1863, loomed, the President was besieged from both sides of the issue. For support and guidance Lincoln turned to his inner circle. In December 1862, the President turned to Rebecca Pomroy.

The nurse recorded her conversation with the President in a letter to a friend. "I am having a hard struggle; this Proclamation is weighing heavily upon me night and day. I shall encounter bitter opposition, but I think good will come of it, and God helping me, I will carry it through," Abraham Lincoln confided to Rebecca Pomroy. In her letter, Rebecca described a man who was weighed down, but defiant. President Lincoln knew that the North was ready for the Emancipation Proclamation, despite the criticism he was convinced that what he was doing was morally right. President Lincoln would express his determination in signing the proclamation, declaring, "If my name ever goes into history it will be for this act, and my whole soul is into it." (224)

During this period, President Abraham Lincoln began to show a public interest in Spiritualism for the first time. In the 1890's, Colonel Simon Kase asserted this claim in an interview published in the *New York Evening Sun* regarding the late President's curiosity about Spiritualism. (225) Colonel Kase's interview gained notoriety within the Spiritualist community and Kase later expanded his narrative in his self-published pamphlet, *The Emancipation Proclamation: How, and by Whom, It was Given to Abraham Lincoln in 1861.*

Spiritualist critic Fayette Hall also included Kase's account published in the *Sun* to support his claims that demonically possessed Spiritualists had influenced Abraham Lincoln to free the slaves and destroy the South. (226) According to Hall, Colonel Kase, an ardent Spiritualist, unknowingly assisted the nefarious plans of the Spiritualists by introducing the President to the celebrated medium J.B. Conklin. (227) Conklin, a prominent trance medium had already tried to get attention from President Abraham Lincoln. Shortly after the inauguration, Conklin received publicity for his claim that Lincoln had attended a séances conducted by the medium in New York. Later that year, the President received a letter transcribed by Conklin which contained the purported message from the spirit of Edward Baker. While there is no evidence to suggest that Lincoln ever replied to the message from his deceased friend, Conklin remained persistent in his goal of meeting the President. To accomplish his goals, Conklin needed a person to introduce him to the President, and used Colonel Simon Kase as his intermediary.

Sometime during late 1862, Kase came to Washington, D.C. on behalf of his nephew's railroad firm to act as a lobbyist. (228) While on a break from his work, Kase decided that he would take a walk to view his old office building. According to Kase, he found that Conklin had set up shop in his old office. While standing outside his former office, Kase asserted that he heard a voice urging him to enter. Upon entering the building, Kase found the medium writing a letter while being in a trance. After returning to his senses, Conklin instructed Kase to take the letter to the President immediately. Though shocked by the nature of the medium's request, the Colonel nevertheless complied with Kase's strange request and had the medium accompany him. (229)

At the White House, Colonel Kase obtained an audience with President Lincoln while leaving the medium to wait in the gentlemen's parlor. (230) After greeting the President, Kase handed Lincoln the letter. "President Lincoln. SIR: I have been sent to you by the spirit world to speak with you upon matters of vital importance to the nation. I cannot return to New York until I have seen you. Yours very respectfully, J.B. CONKLIN," Simon Kase remembered the letter stating. (231) According to Colonel Simon Kase, the President was stunned by the message. "For several minutes after reading the letter, Mr. Lincoln was silent and seemingly plunged in deep thought. Then he asked me what I knew of 'this spiritualism,'" Kase recalled. Surprised by President Lincoln's question, Kase remembered, "I knew very little about it then, but I knew enough to interest the President very greatly in a half hour's conversation." (232)

In Kase's pamphlet, he stated that he informed President Lincoln about his conversion to Spiritualism in the 1850's. (233) According to Colonel Kase, something in his story triggered Lincoln's interest because when the Colonel rose to leave, the President is said to have instructed his visitor, "Send Mr. Conklin to me on Sunday morning at 10 o'clock." (234) With that Kase retired from the President's office and

78

collected the medium from the gentlemen's parlor where the two left for their respective lodgings. (235)

In the *Evening Sun* interview, Simon Kase asserted that the events took place in early 1862, and then in his pamphlet written sometime in the early 1900's Kase proclaimed that the meeting took place in 1861. (236) Kase's memory was likely distorted with the passage of time and by his advancing years. Internal clues within the narrative, such as Kase meeting the Spiritualist medium Nettie Colburn at the Laurie's residence place the events described above as occurring in late 1862. (237)

While it sounds shocking that President Lincoln would summon J.B. Conklin, a Spiritualist medium, for a spur of the moment meeting, this was in keeping with the President's personality. "He has an orbit of his own, and no one can tell where he will be or what he will do, from anything done yesterday," a friend of Lincoln's recorded during the Civil War. (238) To Simon Kase, President Lincoln's willingness to meet with the medium demonstrated that the President was a Spiritualist. To Hall, Colonel Simon Kase was a naïve fool who was used to dupe the President. "But did it never occur to him that Conklin might have had some one in collusion with him. Or that he might have been a ventriloquist, and himself on the lookout for gudgeons," Hall asked. (239)

Continuing his rant, Hall sneered, "And how very innocent and interested Mr. Lincoln was on the subject of spiritualism." (240) According to Hall, the medium was a phony, asserting, "I don't like to say it, but I have pretty good evidence that J.B. Conklin was a trickster, and a cheat." (241) In a later publication, *The Copperhead*, Hall would again assert, "J.B. Conklin was a drunkard, a trickster, and a cheat. A little ventriloquism might have accounted for the mysterious voice." It is unknown if J.B. Conklin ever kept his appointment with the President. After finally getting his chance to meet President Lincoln, Conklin failed to join the Lincolns' circle of friends and acquaintances and he was never mentioned by Nettie Colburn in her memoir. Fayette Hall offered his own interpretation for the medium's disappearance in 1902. "J.B. Conklin, a New York medium, seems to have dropped out of notice after his first interview with the President, as his dissipated habits would preclude his dependence upon him," Hall wrote. (243)

It is very likely that the President had a conversation with Colonel Simon Kase regarding Spiritualism and he might even have invited the Spiritualist medium J.B. Conklin to the White House for a private interview. Seeing that her husband was beginning to have an interest in Spiritualism, Mary Lincoln decided the time was right for her to expand the President's knowledge about Spiritualism.

President Lincoln was famous for his curiosity and his willingness to solicit information regarding topics that interested him. "He was through and indefatigable in his search. He not only went to the root of the question, but dug up the root, and separated and analyzed every fiber of it," William H. Herndon recalled regarding his former law partner's quest for knowledge. (244) Noah Brookes agreed, writing in an 1878 *Scribner's Monthly* article, "Unless very much preoccupied, he never heard any reference to anything that he did not understand without asking further information." (245)

J.B. Conklin was not the only medium who wrote to the President. Even God had a message for the President. Writing through Lydia Smith, God instructed, "Now Abram Lincoln I want you to call together 6 of your best men in the army on the first day possible…I want you to have this Medium present and I will tell you & the 6 beside yourself just what to do that will speedily terminate this Devilish war now existing in your midst." (246) If Lincoln ignored this summons, the Lord threatened dire punishments. "Now do as I tell you or if not you will have to suffer the consequences of not hearing to me," the Lord thundered. (247) Despite these dire predictions, President Lincoln did not summon Lydia Smith to the White House to hear God's message. Soon the President began receiving messages from Spiritualists within the White House.

Besides receiving messages from her children, Mary Lincoln also began to hear political advice from the spirits. Spiritualism offered a way for a politically and economically disenfranchised woman, Nettie Colburn, to exert a fraction of political power and influence in the nation's capital. Impressed by Nettie's talents as a trance medium, Mary Lincoln declared that the President needed to hear what the medium had to say. Shortly after her first meeting with Mary Lincoln, Colburn received a summons to the White House. The First Lady had decided to introduce her husband to Spiritualism within the safety of the family circle at the White House.

These evening events allowed the President the chance to relax and listen to the advice and opinions of his guests. As one anonymous guest remembered, "He talked little, and seemed to prefer others talking to him to talking himself; but, when he spoke, his remarks were always shrewd and sensible." (248) It was at one such evening gathering in late December 1862 that Mary Lincoln invited Nettie Colburn, Cranston and Margaret Laurie, and former Congressman D.E. Somes to the White House for a séance.

"I felt all the natural trepidation of a young girl about to enter the presence of the highest magistrate in our land, being fully impressed with the dignity of his office, and feeling that I was about to meet some superior being; and it was almost with trembling that I entered with my friends the Red Parlor at the White House, at eight o'clock that evening (December 1862)," the medium admitted in her memoir. (249) Whatever the President was expecting, he was clearly amused when he first laid eyes on the young medium. Nettie recalled their first meeting, "Dropping his hand upon my head, he said, in a humorous tone, 'so this is our 'little Nettie' is it, that we heard so much about'" (250)

The First Lady had chosen the perfect medium to introduce to her husband. Mary Lincoln was concerned over the welfare of her husband. Willie's death and the burdens of the Civil War had begun to take its toll on President Lincoln. Young and vigorous when he was elected, two years later the President had visibly aged. The onslaught of pressure brought on by the Emancipation Proclamation and the Union defeat at Fredericksburg added to President Lincoln's strain. After greeting the President and his guests, Nettie entered into a trance. According to Nettie, the spirits offered the President advice regarding the Emancipation Proclamation,

> "With the utmost solemnity and force of manner not to
> abate the terms of the issue, and not to delay its enforce-
> ment as a law beyond the opening of the year; and he was
> assured that it was to be the *crowning event of his admin-*

istration and his life; and that while he was being counseled by strong parties to defer the enforcement of it, hop-
ing to supplant it by other measures and to delay action,
he must in no wise heed such counsel, but stand firm to his
convictions and fearlessly perform the work and fulfill the
mission for which he had been raised up by an overruling
Providence." (251)

According to Nettie, her audience was shocked by her message.
D.E. Somes turned to the President and asked if the pressure the medium
described was accurate. The President confirmed that she was correct.
The medium recorded the President as saying, "Under these circumstances that question is perfectly proper, as we are all friends. *It is taking all*
my nerve and strength to withstand such pressure." (252) While it is impossible to verify the truth of this statement, the President's comment
mirrored his statement to Pomroy that occurred around the same time as
Nettie's séance.

Within the privacy of the White House, President Lincoln could
be remarkably candid—shocking his guests with his remarks. "The conversation, like that of all American official men we have met with, was
unrestrained in the presence of strangers, to a degree perfectly astonishing," a guest wrote about his evening with the Lincolns'. While this

guest was discreet about the topics discussed, "really every man here [Washington, D.C.] appears not only to live in a glass house, but in a re-verberating gallery, and to be absolutely indifferent as to who sees or hears him." (253) After discussing what the spirits had to say, the party disbanded for the evening. According to the medium, the President end-ed the evening by turning to her and declaring, "My child, you possess a very singular gift; but that it is of God, I have no doubt. I thank you for coming here tonight. It is more important than any perhaps can under-stand. I must leave you all now; but I hope I shall see you again." (254)

Historians have largely overlooked President Lincoln's attend-ance at the séances conducted by Nettie Colburn Maynard and others be-cause of the difficultly of verifying the sources. Historian Jay Monaghan commented on Maynard's questionable account, "Such are the details of President Lincoln's first séance, an account which has not lost anything in the telling since Nettie must have been influenced by wishful think-ing." Continuing, Monaghan supported Nettie's recitation of the Presi-dent's recorded comments, stating, "Yet there is nothing in the whole dialogue that indicates that Abraham Lincoln did or said any more than any other President or politician would have done in the same situa-tion." (255)

President Lincoln relied on public opinion to gauge which direction the Northern public was leaning. Historian Jay Monaghan pointed out that while making a momentous decision, "Lincoln is known to have consulted every angle of opinion before embarking on the enterprise." (256) President Lincoln's former law partner, William H. Herndon, bemoaned the President's openness to solicit the opinions of average Americans. "He had great—too great confidence in the common judgment of an uneducated people. He believed that the common people had truths that philosophers never dreamed of; and often appealed to that common judgment of the common people over the shoulders of scientists. I am not saying that he did right. I am only stating what I know to be facts, to be truths," Herndon groused in 1885. (257)

Recognizing that Nettie was a Spiritualist lecturer, President Lincoln would have been aware that she would be spreading her support for the Emancipation Proclamation, under the guise or the reality that she was voicing the spirits' opinion. All the President had to do was to look at his wife to see the impact Spiritualist mediums held over their audiences.

However, this positive affirmation did not make Lincoln a Spiritualist and the President decided to keep his interest in Spiritualism discreet. Mary Lincoln was open in her belief in Spiritualism and shared her experiences with family and friends. Despite finding a companion in Elizabeth Keckly and Rebecca Pomroy, the First Lady was still lonely. The intimacy she once shared with her husband had been disrupted by the Civil War and Willie's death. Mary had a chatty personality and loved to talk; unfortunately, she was not always discreet with those she decided in which share her confidence.

One such individual was Illinois Senator Orville Hickman Browning. The Lincolns had been political friends with the Brownings in Illinois, but since the Lincolns arrival in Washington D.C. there had been a cooling in their relationship. Orville Browning became disappointed when the President failed to offer him a coveted patronage position that he felt he deserved for helping get Lincoln elected. Furthering the estrangement, Browning had became an outspoken critic of the Emancipation Proclamation declaring that the Proclamation would alienate Northern Democrats and that this would cost the Republican Party votes in the next election. (258)

Despite the cooling of relations between Browning and the President, the Senator regularly paid social calls at the White House where he visited both the President and Mary Lincoln. In Orville Browning, Mary Lincoln found a companion to gossip with and discuss the latest revelations from the spirit world. Unbeknownst to Mary Lincoln, Orville

Browning faithfully recorded these private conversations in his diary and in letters to his wife.

On January 1, 1863, Browning recorded his conversation with the First Lady held that day during a carriage ride. "Mrs. Lincoln told me she had been, the night before…out to Georgetown, to see Mrs. Laury, a spiritualist and she had made wonderful revelations to her about her son Willy who had died last winter, and about things on earth," Browning wrote. (259)

"Among other things she revealed that the cabinets were all enemies of the President, working for themselves, and that they would have to be dismissed, and others called to his aid before he had success," Browning concluded. (260) Mary Lincoln had chosen the wrong person to relay her disapproval of her husband's cabinet—even if it was coming from the spirit world. Browning was no longer a loyal supporter of her husband and if he wanted to politically embarrass his friend and the administration he could have revealed to the press the First Lady's inflammatory words.

President Lincoln was interested in Spiritualism, even if that interest did not signify complete belief. Through the séance conducted by Nettie Colburn, the President received validation and support regarding the Emancipation Proclamation. This likely provided a tremendous reassurance for the President who was being overwhelmed by criticism over his decision to enact the proclamation. Lincoln was also an astute enough politician to realize that despite his own opinions regarding the subject, Spiritualism could help the administration. Since the 1850s, Spiritualist mediums had a history of advancing social issues including abolition and women's rights through their lectures, publications, and séances. (261) The President realized that Spiritualism could help the Northern public accept the Emancipation Proclamation and the shifting goal of the Union war effort.

Part Three

"I Could Never Have Smiled Again"

In April 1863, reporter Prior Melton submitted his dispatch to the *Boston Saturday Evening Gazette*. Instead of reporting on the latest political gossip or news from the battlefield, Melton reported on a séance held in the White House. The reporter had gained access to the White House séance due to his friendship with the medium Charles Shockle. According to Melton the President and First Lady were joined by Secretary of the Navy Gideon Welles and Secretary of War Edwin Stanton. The dispatch submitted by Prior Melton to his editors at the was quickly picked up by other newspapers and in a short time the news had spread across the country that President Lincoln was a Spiritualist. The news that President Lincoln had attended a Spiritualist séance at the White House exposed the President to a firestorm of criticism that proved dangerous on the eve of the 1864 election.

Chapter Seven

"It would be hardly advisable for President Lincoln ...to attend a spiritual séance"

President Lincoln was frequently frustrated by those who claimed that they spoke on behalf of divine authority. "Is it not odd that the only channel He could send it by, was the roundabout route by way of that awful city of Chicago?" Lincoln is said to have proclaimed after being visited by an earnest pastor from Chicago. The pastor had come to the President's office proclaiming that he came with "a message to you from our Divine Master." (262) Despite his skepticism, President Lincoln exhibited a curiosity about his wife's faith.

When discussing the Lincolns' attendance at Spiritualist séances, historians maintain that President Lincoln attended only two séances during the Civil War. The primary sources suggest otherwise. Nettie Colburn's memoir documents that President Lincoln frequently attended séances throughout his presidency. "I do...know that he held communications with numerous mediums both at the White House and at other places, and among his mediumistic friends were Charles Foster, Charles Colchester, Mrs. Lucy A. Hamilton, and Charles Redmond," Nettie recorded.

(263) These séances occurred at the White House and in the private dwellings of the mediums, as the February 1863 séance recorded by Nettie Colburn illustrated.

"One morning, early in February, we received a note from Mrs. Lincoln saying she desired us to come over to Georgetown and wished the 'young ladies' to be present," Nettie Colburn Maynard recalled. (264) According to Nettie, upon receiving the note the young medium became controlled by her spirit guide, a 500-year-old Aztec princess called Pinkie. (265) Under the control of Pinkie, Nettie announced that the President would be accompanying his wife to the séance. (266) "Mr. Laurie rather questioned its accuracy; as he said it would be *hardly advisable for President Lincoln to leave the White House to attend a spiritual séance anywhere*; and that he did not consider it 'good policy' to do so," Nettie remembered. (267)

The spirit's pronouncement proved correct. The President had decided to accompany his wife at the last minute. Nettie Colburn later recounted the scene in her memoir, "He came down from a cabinet meeting as Mrs. Lincoln and her friends were about to enter the carriage, and asked them where they were going. She replied, 'To Georgetown; to a circle.' He answered, 'Hold on a moment, I will go with you.'" This shocked his wife who declared to Nettie Colburn, "Yes…and I was never so surprised in my life." (268)

While Mary Lincoln might have been surprised that her husband had wanted to attend the séance, the President's actions are reminiscent of his participation at Mary's mesmerism in 1842. Despite his lifelong interest in the metaphysical, historian Jay Monaghan described Lincoln's appearance at séances as "casual" and "extemporaneous." (269) This statement is not supported by Nettie Colburn's account. Mirroring his involvement at his wife's mesmerism, President Lincoln appeared to be an enthusiastic participant in the séances he attended. Something at the séances triggered the President's interest.

During this period, it was common for Spiritualists to conduct séances like evangelical worship service. After the participants had gathered and assembled around the table, it was typical that certain appropriate hymns would be sung, followed by a reading of Scripture before concluding with a brief prayer. President Lincoln was never comfortable with expressing his religious beliefs within an evangelical perspective.

As a child, Abraham was frequently punished by his father for his scathing impressions of clergymen and would not become a member of his parents' Baptist church. (270) Instead of coaching their séances in the language of the Second Great Awakening, the Lauries embraced a secular Spiritualism. Rather than singing hymns, the Lauries started the séance held in February 1863 by singing old Scottish airs—which were particular favorites of the President's. (271)

After the Scottish airs where sung the séances began. As part of the evening's events the spirits communicated with President Lincoln and advised the President that visit the troops on the front lines in Virginia to approve moral. According to Colburn the spirits instructed Lincoln:

> "Go in person to the front; taking with you your wife and children; leaving behind your official dignity, and all manner of display. Resist the importunities of official dignity, and all manner of display. Resist the importunities of officials to accompany you, and take only such attendants as may be absolutely necessary; avoid the high grade officers, and seek the tents of the private soldiers. Inquire into their grievances; show yourself to be what you are, 'The Father of your People.' Make them feel that you are interested in their sufferings, and that you are not unmindful of the many trials which beset them in their march through the dismal swamps, whereby both their courage and numbers have been depleted." (272)

According to the medium, the President was impressed by this message and remarked, "If that will do any good, it is easily done." (273) As the evening wore on the spirits got frisky and caused a piano to levitate. (274) Levitating objects were common occurrences during séances during this period as evidence that the spirits were present. (275) The Lauries were famous for their levitating piano that would rise up off the ground while their daughter, Belle Miller, played. During the séance the piano—either through some trickery or the power of the spirits— levitated and that the President in a spirit of jest decided to sit on the piano.

According to Nettie Colburn, "The President, with a quaint smile, said, 'I think we can hold down that instrument.' Whereupon he climbed upon it, sitting with his legs dangling over the side, as also did Mr. Somes, S.P. Kase, and a soldier in the uniform of a major…from the Army of the Potomac. The piano, notwithstanding this enormous added weight, continued to wabble (sic) about until the sitters were glad 'to vacate the premises.'" (276)

The President was amused by the adventure and was convinced that there was no trickery involved. After the President had completed his investigation of the piano, D.E. Somes jokingly remarked to Lincoln, "When I have related to my acquaintances, Mr. President, that which I have experienced tonight, they will say, with a knowing look and wise demeanor, 'You were psycho-analogized, and as a matter of fact (*versus* fancy) you *did not see* what you in reality *did see*.'" To which Lincoln replied, "You should bring such person here, and when the piano seems to rise, have him slip his foot under the leg and be *convinced* (doubtless) by the weight of *evidence* resting upon his *understanding*." (277) In the 1890s the levitating piano entered the public's imagination after Colonel

Simon Kase was interviewed by the *New York Sun* in the early 1890's. (278)

President Lincoln was a physically fit man who frequently displayed his physical abilities in moments of levity and relaxation. (279) Lincoln was known for his curiosity. When Lincoln saw a puzzle, he did everything in his power to find the answer, even if it included taking Tad's toys apart to see how they worked. (280) The séance concluded and the Lincolns' returned to the burdens of the war. "I believe that Mr. Lincoln was satisfied and convinced that the communications he received through me were wholly independent of my volition, and in every way superior to any manifestation that could have been given me as a *physical* being," Nettie Colburn affirmed in her memoir. (281)

Nettie Colburn's memoir is not the only source testifying to President Abraham Lincoln's attendance at Spiritualist séances. In 1885, Jack Laurie, Cranston and Margaret Laurie's son, wrote to the Spiritualist newspaper, *The Religio-Philosophical Journal* about the events that he had witnessed in his family's parlor during the Civil War. According to Jack Laurie, "I have very often seen Mr. Lincoln at my father's house engaged in attending circles for spiritual phenomena, and generally Mrs. Lincoln was with him." (282)

Jack Laurie's account provides valuable information about the Lincolns' interest in Spiritualism and their visits to the Lauries' Georgetown residence from 1862 to 1863. "The practice of attending circles by Mr. Lincoln at my father's house continued from early in 1862, to late in 1863, and during portions of the time such visits were very frequent....I remember well one evening when Nettie Colburn, a medium, was present, Mr. Lincoln seemed very deeply interested in the proceedings and asked a great many questions of the spirits." (283) Jack Laurie is incorrect when he stated that President Lincoln began attending Spiritualist séances at his parents at the beginning of 1862.

Beside's corroborating Nettie Colburn's memoir, Jack Laurie's testimony provided insight into what occurred during the séances the Lincolns attended. As Jack Laurie recalled, "I have on several occasions seen Mr. Lincoln at a circle at my father's house, apparently by spiritual forces, that he became partially entranced, and I have heard him make remarks while in that condition, in which he spoke of his deceased son Willie, and said that he saw him." (284) Jack Laurie's memory of President Lincoln's visions of Willie is remarkably similar to the President's conversation with the Army officer in 1862 in which Lincoln admitted that he still sensed Willie's presence around him. (285)

Jack Laurie's account mirrors Nettie Colburn Maynard's assertion that President Lincoln was deeply interested in the topics discussed during her séances. "I have on several occasions seen Mr. Lincoln take notes of what was said by mediums," Jack recalled in his 1885 letter. At times the séances held at the Lauries' home could become rather rambunctious affairs. "At one circle, I remember that a heavy table was being raised and caused to dance about the room by what purported to be spirits. Mr. Lincoln laughed heartily and said to my father, 'Never mind, Cranston, if they break the table, I will give you a new one,'" Jack remembered. (286)

Concluding his letter, Jack Laurie provided a tantalizing clue into the religious beliefs of President Lincoln. "On one occasion, I remember well of hearing my father ask Mr. Lincoln, if he believed the phenomena he had witnessed was caused by spirits, and Mr. Lincoln replied, that he did so believe," Jack Laurie asserted. (287)

Chapter Eight

"I believe that, whether it comes from spirit or human"

The news that President Abraham Lincoln was attending Spiritualist séances gradually became public by the summer of 1863. This ignited a controversy that has not faded. Foes of the President would use the Lincolns' involvement with Spiritualism to discredit the President's policy and used it as evidence that both Abraham and Mary Lincoln were mentally unsound. Even an acquaintance of the Lauries' would condemn the President for his interest in Spiritualism. Fayette Hall, an embittered Connecticut Democrat vigorously disagreed with President Lincoln's politics. "He was ignorant, superstitious and vain, but an ambitious man. A fortune-teller had told him in early life that he was going to be President of the United States, and when spiritualism was introduced he began consulting those of that faith," Hall wrote. (288)

In his political exposé published in 1890, *The Secret and Political History of the Rebellion*, Fayette Hall claimed that during the summer of 1863 he had been a guest in the Lauries' Georgetown home. "Where I remained for three weeks, with my eyes and ears open, and with the opportunity of learning some of the secret working of the time, so that on my return to New Haven was prepared to dispute Mr. Lincoln's right to the title of 'Honest Abe,'" Hall proclaimed. (289)

Fayette Hall did not limit his invective to the President. Regarding Nettie Colburn, Hall dismissed the young woman as a "child" and attributed her Spiritual messages to the coaching of her handlers. "But Nettie was a bright little girl, and capable of quite an effort, and she had good instructors," Hall claimed. (290) During his stay in the Lauries' home, Hall asserted, "As to little Nettie Maynard, she was a bright child of, I should think, not more than twelve years of age, and a ward of Mr. Laurie's. As to her wonderful mediumship I saw or heard nothing. But then it was warm weather and Judge Wattles [Colburn's patron according to Hall], her spiritual congress, was not present." (291)

In his book, Fayette Hall got a number of details wrong. First, Nettie Colburn asserted that she was in her early 20's during the Civil War. Furthermore, Nettie Colburn was not the Lauries' ward. Hall is an unreliable source as his book is full of wild and unsubstantiated claims. For instance, Hall began his exposé by asserting that President Lincoln received the Republican nomination in 1860 due to a cabal of Spiritualists and that throughout the war the President employed Spiritualists to communicate with the spirit of Attila the Hun who guided Lincoln in his nefarious plan of becoming a dictator. (292) Amazingly, Fayette Hall

asserted that he did not object to Spiritualism, asserting, "I should state

that it is not spiritualism that I am discussing or meddling with, or any

other religious belief that does not meddle with the rights and privileges

of others...But there I stop, as I have never discovered any benefit to be

derived from it. Let the theory be true or false, I have no objection to

others enjoying it." (293) To the horror of some observers the President

appeared to enjoy attending séances with his wife.

Throughout her memoir, Nettie Colburn took great pains to assert

that even though President Lincoln did frequently attend Spiritualist

gatherings, she did not claim that President Lincoln was a Spiritualist.

"It has frequently been stated that Mr. Lincoln was a Spiritualist. That

question is left open for general judgment," Nettie wrote. (294) Instead,

the medium left it up to the reader to form their own opinion.

Regarding the First Lady's belief in Spiritualism, the medium was

more definitive stating, "It is also true that Mrs. Lincoln was more enthu-

siastic regarding the subject than her husband, and openly and avowedly

professed herself connected with the new religion." (295) Mary Lin-

coln's belief brought a number of mediums to the White House.

Nettie Colburn was not the only Spiritualist medium who came to

the White House. Mary Lincoln employed a variety of Spiritualist mediums besides Nettie Colburn during the Civil War. One séance conducted by another medium would garner national attention. In April 1863, the Lincolns hosted a séance in the Red Room conducted by Charles E. Shockle. (296) For this séance Abraham and Mary Lincoln invited Sectary of the Navy Gideon Welles and Sectary of War Edwin Stanton.

Charles Shockle was accompanied by his friend Prior Melton, a reporter for the *Boston Saturday Evening Gazette*, who preserved the evening's events in an article for his newspaper. (297) "A few evenings since, Abraham Lincoln, President of the United States, was induced to give a spiritual soirée in the Crimson Room [Red Room] at the White House, to test the wonderful alleged supernatural powers of Mr. Charles E. Shockle," Melton reported in his official account. (298)

According to Melton, the spirit circle began with the assembled party gathering around a table. Shortly after the circle had commenced, the President was called away from the parlor, much to the spirits displeasure. "The spirits, which had apparently assembled to convince him of their power, gave visible tokens of their displeasure at the President's absence, by pinching Mr. Stanton's ears and twitching Mr. Welles's beard," Melton recorded. (299)

President Lincoln's absence was not long and the séance continued with the spirits demonstrating their powers by physically lifting items around the parlor. (300) After the spirits had established that they were present, Schockle produced paper and pencil which he laid on the table and covered with a handkerchief. According to Melton Prior, within moments a message appeared on the paper from Henry Knox, the first Secretary of War under George Washington. Amused, President Lincoln asked if it was possible for Knox to tell him how much longer the war was going to last.

Within moments the following answer appeared: "Washington, Lafayette, Franklin, Wilberforce, Napoleon and myself have held frequent consultations on this point. There is something which our spiritual eyes cannot detect which appears well formed. Evil has come at times by removal of men from high positions, and there are those in retirement whose abilities should be made useful to hasten the end. Napoleon says, concentrate your forces upon one point; Lafayette thinks that the rebellion will die of exhaustion; Franklin sees the end approaching, as the South must give up for want of mechanical ability to compete against Northern mechanics. Wilberforce sees hope only in a negro army.— KNOX." (301)

This rambling message amused the President. "Well opinions differ among the saints as well as among the sinners. They don't seem to understand running the machines among the celestials much better than we do," Lincoln exclaimed. The President then used the spirit's disjointed message as a pointed critique of the often contradicting advice he received from his cabinet officials. "Their talk and advice sound very much like the cabinet—don't you think so Mr. Welles?" Lincoln asked. (302) Cleary uncomfortable with the new direction the evening was taking, Welles fumbled for an answer. "Well, I don't know—I will think the matter over, and see what conclusions to arrive at," Welles feebly answered. (303)

Fortunately for the beleaguered Secretary Welles, Schockle and the spirits picked this moment to continue with their demonstrations. The President asked the medium to ask the spirits about the CSS *Alabama*. The answer came in an impressive feat of physical mediumship in which Melton Prior asserted that the assembled party saw the ship moving across the ocean reflected in the mirror that hung over the fireplace mantel. "Well, Mr. Shockle, I have seen strange things and heard rather odd remarks; but nothing which convinces me, except the pictures, that there is anything very heavenly about this," Lincoln proclaimed.

Before the séance concluded, Abraham Lincoln requested that Charles Schockle contact the spirit of Stephen Douglas. Impressed with Douglas's pronouncement the President concluded, "I believe that, whether it comes from spirit or human." (304) The séance quickly became public knowledge when other Northern newspapers picked up Melton's article, usually under the headline, "Spiritualism at the White House." (305)

Spiritualists and anti-Spiritualist used the White House séances conducted by Charles Schockle as evidence that President Lincoln had converted to Spiritualism. One virulent anti-Spiritualist, David Quinn seized on the publicity of the President's interest in the faith to publish his anti-Lincoln and anti-Spiritualist book *Interior Causes of the War: The Nation Demonized, and it's President a Spirit-Rapper* in 1863.

An Ohio Democrat, Quinn used the pages of his book to assert that the Civil War was caused by demonic spirits who possessed Northern Spiritualist to do their evil deeds by influencing the President. "The war which is upon us, these spirits have induced, by preparing the minds of men for its inauguration, and now, through a president and his advisers, whom they control, they are hurrying the country on to its destruction," Quinn intoned. (306) For Quinn the reports emerging out of the White House that President Lincoln and members of his cabinet were attending Spiritualist séances only enforced his claims.

"Mr. Lincoln, with his aiders and abettors, has assumed great responsibilities in thus revolutionizing the government; but unlike our old fashioned presidents, who were compelled to consult the constitution, he has, in a secret hole of the White House, a *rapping* table, which discourses sweeter music than ever issued from Hamlet's pipe. It is law, constitution and gospel; and the great magical power which gathers armies, presages events, equalizes whites and negroes, and converts paper into gold. Washington, Jefferson, and Jackson, Caesar, Hannibal, Napoleon, Wellington, and all other great men of history, wake from their slumbers and protrude their counsels through it; direct the plans of battles, the windings of anacondas, the policy of proclamations, and the movement of armies; so that a new dispensation looms up around the present power, while laws and constitutions flee before the mystical light, as ragged relics of the vulgar past. Delphos had her oracles, Olympus her enchantments; but all now sink to insignificance before the superior powers of this wonderful table," Quinn thundered with overwrought dramatics. (307)

In an amazing conclusion, Thomas Quinn, much like Fayette Hall, claimed: "But let it not be supposed, in view of these strictures, that we censure Mr. Lincoln for believing that spirits actually communicate; this would be grossly unjust, for instead of censuring him for such belief, he has our full approval in this particular, for we know the point to be one in regard to which he is much in advance of the great body of men, who think themselves much wiser. But the point of which we disapprove

106

is his placing any confidence in what spirits tell him; and our censure are for his attempting to administer our government under mysterious and unknown councils. The people's government should be directed by the people, and not by spiritual communications," Quinn concluded. (308) This would be only the beginning of the harsh criticism that President Lincoln received for his interest in Spiritualism.

The publication of a British song "The Dark Séance Polka" composed by J.H. Addison hints that the knowledge of President Lincoln's interest in Spiritualism had spread to Europe. (309) Since Spiritualism emerged as a growing religious movement, song writers had produced works that capitalized on Spiritualist beliefs. In 1853 songwriters T.E. Carrett and W.E. Rossington capitalized on Spiritualism with the balled "Spirit Rappings." "Softly, softly, hear the rustle / Of the Spirits airy wings; / They are coming down to mingle / Once again with earthly things, / With their rapping, and their tapping, / Rap-tap-tap to wake our napping," the song intoned. (310) Even the sheet music cover reflected the songs sentimental lyrics, a family, complete with a dreamy-eyed young girl are gathered around a table trying to communicate with the spirits. While such songs as "Spirit Rappings" endorsed Spiritualism, not all song writers supported the religion as seen with "The Dark Séance Polka."

In the illustration, an audience is witnessing a séance preformed by a pair of fraudulent mediums. The mediums have darkened the room and have slipped out of their boots and are dancing around the room playing on musical instruments. Sitting in the center is bearded man with an unlit candle apparently unaware that the mediums are leaping around him in their stockings. What makes the man so intriguing is that the man appears to be a badly drawn caricature of President Lincoln. (311) In appearance, the illustration for "The Dark Séance Polka" was meant to mock the President and his wife for attending Spiritualist séances. In the right hand corner of the illustration is a well dressed plump woman who could be the artist's stand-in caricature for Mary Lincoln whose image was less well known in Europe as compared to her husband's.

Historians and writers who have studied the image believed that the bearded man was in fact a caricature of Abraham Lincoln. In 1963, the editors of the publication *Lincoln Lore* included the illustration to accompany an article on the Lincolns' involvement with Spiritualism. According to the article the illustration which is housed in the Lincoln Memorial University special collections, "bears the title 'Abraham Lincoln and the Spiritualists.'" (312) Unfortunately, the original sheet music does not feature that caption and it is unclear if that is the official title of the illustration or if that is the title a librarian cataloged the image when it was entered into the Lincoln Memorial University library.

Chapter Nine

"Very close spirits themselves"

As the months passed, Mary Lincoln and Nettie Colburn formed a symbiotic relationship dependent on the mediums ability to channel the spirits. An incident that occurred during the Battle of Chancellorsville in May 1863 perfectly illustrated their relationship. Because of the services that Nettie preformed for the Lincolns and was trusted by the First Lady, the medium was granted full access to the White House. This included the freedom to obtain flowers from the White House greenhouse. According to Nettie, one morning, the medium decided to obtain some flowers to bring to her father and brother who were patients at one of the countless military hospitals in the capital. "Intending to visit him, I went by permission of Mrs. Lincoln to the White House hothouse to obtain a bouquet of flowers for him," Nettie recalled. (313)

Arriving at the private entrance of the White House with her friend Parthenia "Parnie" Hannum, the young women expected to be given a pre-cut bouquet. Instead, Nettie found Mrs. Cuthbert, the White House housekeeper waiting for her. "Oh, my dear young ladies," Mrs.

Cuthbert exclaimed, "the madam is deestracted. Come to her, I beg of you. She wants you very much." (314) Following the French born housekeeper into the President's private quarters, Nettie and her friend found the First Lady in her wrapper with her hair down frantically pacing up and down her room. Turning to the medium, Mary Lincoln explained the reason for her distress. The Battle of Chancellorsville was raging and the President had just received a telegram announcing that the Union army was in the process of being destroyed with numerous officers dead. "Will you sit down a few moments and see if you can get anything from 'beyond?'" the desperate First Lady pleaded. (315)

Not wishing to pass up such an opportunity to display her skill, Nettie complied with Mary Lincoln's request. Nettie then preformed a short séance which calmed Mary's frayed nerves. Upon the conclusion of Nettie's impromptu séance, President Lincoln entered his wife's bedroom. Mary Lincoln was enthusiastic over what Nettie had just done for her and according to the medium, "Mrs. Lincoln instantly began to tell him what had been said." (316) Seizing the moment, Nettie performed another séance for the benefit of the President and Mrs. Cuthbert.

According to the medium the message she relayed to Abraham and Mary Lincoln from the other side brought reassurance that the apocalyptic tone of the telegram had been false. "My friend said she had never seen me more impressive or convincing when under control," Nettie bragged in her memoir. (317)

Grateful for the reassuring message, Mary Lincoln expressed her gratitude by giving the women large bouquets of flowers. "I need not say that our hands were well filled with flowers when we left the White House," Nettie concluded. (318) This incident illustrated the type of relationship Mary Lincoln had with the medium. Mary Lincoln relayed on Nettie for her skills as a medium and only brought her into the White House to employ Nettie to do a séance for her. Nettie in turn complied with the First Lady's request due to the material advantages it brought her. Despite remaining discreet, Nettie's activities in the White House became well known within the Spiritualist community.

President Lincoln received the congratulations of Spiritualist writer John W. Edmonds on his conversion to Spiritualism in a letter dated June 1, 1863. In his letter Edmonds declared to Lincoln, "Amid my consideration of that subject I was assured, from a source which I had learned to put a good deal of confidence in, that we should have a Spiritualist as a President." (319)

Continuing Edmonds gushed, "I have heard & read in various ways, without surprise that you, Sir, are so far interested in the subject, as to have upon its investigation." (320) Edmonds then offered President

Lincoln copies of his books he had written about Spiritualism. (321) As a writer of Spiritualist literature, John W. Edmonds needed a prominent follower who would lend Spiritualism creditability. In the North in 1863, there was no one more prominent than Abraham Lincoln, President of the United States. As the year progressed, even the President's close friends would begin to comment on Lincoln's interests.

On October 26, 1863, Abraham Lincoln received a note from his close friend Joshua Speed. Lincoln had first met Speed upon his arrival in Springfield, Illinois in 1840 and the two had struck up a close friendship. (322) By the time of the Civil War, Lincoln's and Speed's relationship had lost some of its former luster. In part this was caused by the burden of the war which had placed a strain on all of the President's personal relationships.

Further straining their friendship was that Speed had returned to his birth state of Kentucky where he owned slaves. Despite professing his loyalty to the Union war effort, Speed had openly disagreed with his former roommate's political policy. (323) Throughout the war Speed made periodic visits to the nation's capital and it was during one of these visits that he decided to write a letter of introduction for the medium Nettie Colburn and her friend Anna Cosby.

"My very good friend Mrs. Cosby and Miss Netty Colburn her friend desire an interview with you," Speed wrote. (324) President Lincoln was already well acquainted with the medium and Anna Cosby. Nettie had just made her acquaintance with Speed in the fall of 1863 upon her return to Washington, D.C. after taking a trip to New York to visit her parents. (325) At the time, Nettie was residing at the home of her friend Anna Cosby whose husband had just lost his position as consul to Switzerland amid accusations of associating with Confederate officials while at his post in Geneva. (326)

The medium was concerned that because of her friend's fall from grace her access to the Lincoln White House would be affected. This would have hurt Nettie's budding political power. Her access to the President and First Lady had become well known throughout Washington, D.C and people flocked to Nettie to beg her to plead their case with the President. The medium needed to be able to see Lincoln on the behalf of these claimants.

One of these petitioners, Colonel Morgan H. Chrysler had summoned Nettie back to the capital from her vacation in New York to aide him in acquiring the command of his brigade. "He had confidence in my power to reach the President, and he had also confidence in the unseen powers that controlled me, and he earnestly requested that I should make the effort in his behalf, offering to defray all expenses, which he did," Nettie stated. (327) In an attempt to ensure her admittance to the President, Nettie likely asked Joshua Speed to write her a letter of introduction. Joshua Speed, impressed by a séance Nettie Colburn had done for him gladly, performed the task. "It will I am sure be some relief from the tedious round of office seekers to see two such agreeable ladies," Speed wrote.

Joshua Speed was quick to add that they were mediums gushing, "They are both mediums & believe in the spirits—and are I am quite sure very close spirits themselves." In the postscript, Speed added, "Mrs. Cosby says she is not a medium though I am quite sure she is or should be." (328) This letter has confused historians who have taken the letter as proof that Joshua Speed was the one who first introduced Nettie to the Lincolns. A careful examination of Nettie's memoir corrects this error and places the letter into context.

The medium's concerns were unfounded. Upon her arrival at the White House, she was admitted into the President's office where Lincoln gave her a friendly welcome. "How do you do, Miss Nettie?—glad to see you back among us," President Lincoln announced. (329) Though unable to help Nettie, the President appeared happy to see the young medium again and directed her to take the matter to the Secretary of the

War. (330) Undeterred, Nettie visited Edwin Stanton and successfully persuaded the cantankerous Secretary to grant her request. (331)

Though President Lincoln did have an interest in Spiritualism as demonstrated by his attendance at séances, he tried to keep his interest quiet. The newspaper article written by Prior Melton had produced negative publicity and inspired Thomas Quinn to publish his attack on the Lincoln presidency. The President's attendance at one séance had caused a firestorm of criticism. If it was known that the he had attended more than several séances, Lincoln's creditability and his hopes for re-election would have been placed in jeopardy. Mary Lincoln saw no danger in her husband's position regarding Spiritualism. She once informed Nettie, "But I tell Mr. Lincoln, if we are going to take spirits' advice, let us do it fully, and then there can be no responsibility resting with us if it fails." (332) Needless to say Lincoln did not share his wife's view on this issue and strove to keep the attendance at séances secret.

This secrecy even extended to Nettie Colburn Maynard who was warned by her inner circle to keep silent. "Mr. Somes frequently warned me that it would be unwise to talk to newspaper men, or to answer any of the many inquires that were constantly made regarding the subject of our Presidential séances—saying impressively, 'Do not make the matters public property in any such manner at the present time,'" Nettie remembered. (333) President Lincoln could not politically afford to have the Northern public know how active he and Mary were in Spiritualism. "Again, had he declared an open belief in the subject, he would have been pronounced insane and probably incarcerated," Nettie declared in 1891. (334) Thomas Quinn also agreed with the medium writing in 1863, "Mr. Lincoln's faith, not his learning, has made him mad; and so deep is that madness, that could the facts which have influenced his policy be ascertained, he could, we have no doubt, be proved a madman on a fair trial, under the writ of lunacy." (335)

Chapter Ten

"A Colchester Sitting"

As Mary Lincoln turned to the capital's growing Spiritualist community, the First Lady became vulnerable to charlatans who tried to use her for economic and political advantage. One such charlatan who targeted the First Lady was the English medium Lord Charles J. Colchester. According to Noah Brooks, Elizabeth Keckly "had induced Mrs. Lincoln to listen to the artful tales of a so-called spiritual medium who masqueraded under the name of Colchester, and who pretended to be the illegitimate son of an English duke." (336) Whatever Keckly witnessed during Colchester's séance, it so impressed her that she recommended the medium to the First Lady. (337)

Historian Stephen Mansfield disagrees with Brooks' identification of Elizabeth Keckly as the person who introduced the First Lady to Colchester. "There may have been some racism in this," Mansfield writes. Arguing that Spiritualism was the sole possession of upper-class whites claiming, "Elizabeth Keckly could have done no more than encourage Mary Lincoln in what she already experienced with her white, upper-class friends." (338) The First Lady was intrigued by the medium's reputation and invited him to perform a séance for her.

"By playing on her motherly sorrows, Colchester actually succeeded in inducing Mrs. Lincoln to receive him in the family residence at the Soldiers' Home, where, in a darkened room, he pretended to produce messages from the boy by means of scratches on the wainscoting and taps on the walls and furniture," Noah Brooks wrote in his memoir. (339) As she had with Rebecca Pomroy and Oliver Browning, Mary Lincoln shared her faith in Spiritualism with Noah Brooks. The California reporter had also experienced a devastating loss when his wife died in 1862. (340) Like Rebecca Pomroy, Brooks remained skeptical and declined the First Lady's invitation to attend a White House séance featuring the English medium. (341)

The Lincolns were intrigued by the manifestations that Colchester produced during his séances. President Lincoln wanted to get the opinion of Dr. Joseph Henry, head of the Smithsonian Intuition and the country's premier scientist. On the behest of the President, Dr. Henry received the medium in his office at the Smithsonian. Eager to gather another convert, Colchester summoned the spirits and raps filled the office. Dr. Henry, though, was unimpressed. "I do not know how you make these sounds, but this I perceive very clearly—they do not come from the room but from your person," Joseph Henry informed the medium. (342)

Henry's observation's proved correct. While on a train, Henry met a

man who confessed to the scientist that he sold instruments to Colchester

and other charlatan mediums to aid them in their presentations. (343) It

is unknown if Dr. Henry shared his discoveries with the President. As it

would turn out, it would be Noah Brooks who would reveal Lord Col-

chester's true character to the Lincolns'.

Shortly after declining his invitation to attend one of Mary Lin-

coln's séances, Noah Brooks changed his mind. "I received an invitation

to invest one dollar and attend 'a Colchester sitting' at the house of a

Washington gentleman who was a profound believer in this pretentious

seer. To gratify my curiosity, I paid the entrance fee, and, accompanied

by a trusty friend, went to the séance," Brooks recounted. (344) Assem-

bled with his skeptical friend, the reporter was not impressed by what he

witnessed. Colchester began the séance after all the lights in the parlor

were extinguished and all the assembled participants had joined hands.

Only then would the spirits announce their presence by producing

manifestations that caused musical instruments to play on their own ac-

cord. Suspecting trickery, Brooks loosened his hands and in his account,

"grasping in the direction of the drum-beat, grabbed a very solid and

fleshy hand in which was held a bell that was being thumped on a drumhead." (345) Determined to end this charade Brooks called for his friend

to turn on a light, but before his friend could act the investigative reporter

received a blow to the head with the drum. "When the gas was finally

lighted, the singular spectacle was presented of 'the son of the duke'

firmly grasped by a man whose forehead was covered with blood, while

the arrested scion of nobility was glowering at the drum and bells which

he still held in his hands," Brooks gleefully recalled. (346) The séance

ended with the exposed medium storming out of the room.

Despite being exposed as a fraud, Charles Colchester continued to

be a thorn in Noah Brooks' side. Instead of attacking Brooks again, the

medium changed tactics and decided to go after Mary Lincoln. Noah

Brooks was a well-known friend of the President and it was conceivable

that Colchester believed that the reporter had been sent to the séance on

the behest of President Lincoln.

A few days after the interrupted séance, Noah Brooks received a

note from Mary Lincoln requesting that he come to the White House as

soon as possible. Arriving at the White House, Brooks found a frazzled

First Lady. Mary Lincoln showed Brooks a note she had received from

Charles Colchester, "in which he requested that she should procure for

him from the War Department a pass to New York, and intimated that in case she refused he might have some unpleasant things to say to her." (347)

Infuriated, Noah Brooks concocted a plan to expose the medium. Brooks arraigned for Mary Lincoln to invite Colchester to the White House the next day. At the appointed time, Charles Colchester arrived at the White House probably with the expectation that he was going to get his pass. After formally introducing Noah Brooks to the medium, Mary Lincoln withdrew from the room. "Going up to Colchester, I lifted the hair from the scar on my forehead, yet unhealed, and said, 'Do you recognize this?'" Brooks demanded. "You know that I know you are a swindler and a humbug. Get out of this house and out of this city at once. If you are in Washington to-morrow afternoon at this time, you will be in the old Capitol prison," Brooks threatened. (348)

Realizing that he had crossed the wrong person, Charles Colchester fled the White House and never harassed the First Lady again. Despite this exposure to a fraudulent medium, Mary Lincoln's faith in Spiritualism remained unshattered and she continued to try to convert her family and friends.

In December 1863, Mary Lincoln's favorite half-sister, Emilie Todd Helm, came to Washington, D.C. to visit the Lincolns. Like her older sister Emilie had suffered a devastating loss when her husband died while serving in the Confederate Army. Regardless of the controversy of hosting a Confederate sympathizer, President Lincoln invited Emilie to the White House in December 1863 so that the sisters could grieve together. (349) During Emilie visit, Mary decided to share with her sister her belief in Spiritualism. Following Emilie into her bedroom one evening Mary announced:

> "I want to tell you, Emilie, that one may not be wholly without comfort when our loved ones leave us. When my noble little Willie was first taken from me, I felt that I had fallen into a deep pit without a ray of light anywhere. If I had not felt the spur of necessity urging me to cheer Mr. Lincoln, whose grief was as great as my own, I could never have smiled again and if Willie did not come to comfort me I would still be drowned in tears, and while I long to touch him, to hold him in my arms, and still grieve that he has no future in this world that I might watch with a proud mother's heart—he lives, Emilie!...He comes to me every night, and stands at the foot of my bed with the same sweet, adorable smile he has always had; he does not always come alone; little Eddie is sometimes with him and twice he has come with our brother Alec, he tells me he loves his Uncle Alec (350) and is with him most of the time. You cannot dream of the comfort this gives me. When I thought of my little son in immensity, alone, without his mother to direct him, no one to hold his little hand in loving guidance, it nearly broke my heart. (351)

This declaration by Mary Lincoln perfectly illustrated why she found Spiritualism appealing. After Willie's death, she had fallen into a "deep pit," but only through Spiritualism had Mary found comfort through contacting her dead children. Through her dreams or visions of

123

Willie and Eddie, Mary Lincoln was convinced that her sons were in heaven waiting for the day that the family would be re-united. Adding to Mary's comfort her vision confirmed for her that her sons were not alone in heaven, but were being cared for by a loving family member. This proved to be too much for Emilie Helm who recorded in her diary, "It *is* unnatural and abnormal." (352) Despite facing the displeasure of their family, the Lincolns' continued to pursue their interest in Spiritualism.

Six months after receiving John W. Edmonds request that the President accept his books on Spiritualism, President Lincoln received another letter, this time from Senator Edwin D. Morgan regarding Edmonds' offer. Morgan requested that the President, "please read the letter of Judge Edmonds and return it to me that I may tell him you will accept of his Books." (353) President Lincoln finally responded and accepted Edmonds' book offer. "Will Senator Morgan please present my compliments to Judge Edmonds, & say to him the books will be gratefully accepted by me," Lincoln stated to Morgan on January 16, 1864. (354)

Why did President Lincoln decide to accept Edmonds offer? John W. Edmonds' first wrote to President Lincoln in June of 1863 offering the President copies of his books. At the time, the President ignored the offer which prompted Senator Morgan to write to President Lincoln again on Edmonds' behalf. It is possible to deduce that his wife's interest in Spiritualism was having a powerful impact on him. President Lincoln's acceptance of Edmonds' book suggests that the President possessed an interest in Spiritualism.

As this correspondence suggests President Lincoln took great pains to keep his interest in Spiritualism discreet. President Lincoln was an astute politician who realized that it was easy for his private mail to land in the wrong hands. In fact, when, President Lincoln communicated with his family during his term in office it was only through telegraph that went through a secure War Department line that could not be tapped by the press. (355) The fact that President Lincoln requested John W. Edmonds to send him books about Spiritualism suggested that the President wanted to read more about the topic.

During the Civil War, President Lincoln had little leisure time. He was not going to waste his time reading about a subject in which he had no interest. His attendance at séances and his perusal of Spiritualist literature proved that President Lincoln had an active interest in Spiritualism—just like he had 20 years earlier when he witnessed his wife's mesmerism. Unlike Mary Lincoln, the President realized the political damage that could be done if his interest in Spiritualism continued to be bandied about in the press and he tried to remain discreet about his interest.

President Lincoln had a valid reason for keeping his interest in Spiritualism discreet because the new religion was about to be attacked in the nation's capitol. Nettie Colburn detailed the events in her memoir, "During the early part of the winter of 1863 and 1864, a woman by the name of Smith came to Washington upon the subject of Spiritualism." At first Smith was welcomed into Washington's Spiritualist society which embraced her lectures as a way of spreading the faith. "She obtained a hall which was quickly filled with a crowd of eager listeners," Nettie chronicled, "to whom it soon became apparent that she was half deranged." (356)

Smith was not the only Spiritualist lecturer that proved controversial. Itinerant medium Father Beeson packed audiences at the Odd Fellows Hall where he wowed audiences with communications from the spirit of Judge Dean, a noted defender of fugitive slaves before the Civil War. The public was receptive to Father Beeson's pronouncements until he announced that he had received a message from the spirit of an African American man who informed the medium that in Heaven blacks occupied the chief seats next to God. (357)

Horrified over Smith's and Beeson's behavior, Washington's Spiritualists went on damage control and sought out Nettie for assistance. "The Spiritualists of Washington were greatly mortified at having their religious belief thus caricatured, and a gentleman called on Mr. Somes, at whose house I was then stopping and making known his errand asked to see and talk with me," Colburn recorded. (358) The gentleman had come to see Nettie about arranging a lecture to explain the true meaning of Spiritualism to the public. "Mr. Somes introduced me, saying that he represented a number of Spiritualists who had been exceedingly morti-fied at the notoriety given to their religious belief by this crazy woman, and that they desired to get up a public lecture and have me speak for them," Nettie noted. (359)

After some deliberation, Nettie agreed to return to her roots as a public speaker and participate in the lecture. The lecture proved to be a success. After being introduced by the Revered John Pierpont, Nettie spoke to a packed audience. "The interest the subject had awakened in the public mind was apparent from the crowded audience that had assem-bled to meet us," Nettie remembered. (360) The capital's residents had paid a heavy toll during the Civil War and Nettie's hopeful message more than likely brought comfort to her audience.

"We were heard with every mark of respect and attention, and more than one person remarked, *'If this is Spiritualism, it is the most comforting and rational religious belief I ever heard. I would like to know more of it,'*" Nettie proclaimed. (361) Following this lecture more of the capital's residents joined Mary Lincoln in her belief in Spiritualism.

Throughout 1864 Mary Lincoln continued to summon Nettie and her Spiritualists friends to the White House. Shortly after Nettie's public lecture, the medium was invited to the White House to show off her talents for the First Lady's friends. Mary Lincoln declared she had a friend she wanted Nettie to meet, but she wanted to test the medium's powers and would not tell her who the guest was. Instead, Mary decided that Nettie's spirit guide Pinkie should be able to guess the true identity of the mysterious guest. (362)

Naturally, according to Nettie the undefeatable Pinkie correctly guessed that the guest was a military officer who turned out to be none other than General Daniel Sickles. (363) What made this séance stand out, besides the presence of the Union Army's most notorious general, was that in a rare moment of bravado Nettie Colburn gave herself credit for the creation of the Freedman's Bureau. Following President Lincoln's death, Spiritualists tried to give credit for the Emancipation Proclamation to Nettie Colburn's ministrations. This claim troubled the medium and her husband for the rest of their lives. "Mr. Maynard is very anxious that the people should know that his wife never claimed that through her was dictated the Emancipation Proclamation," wrote the

Maynards' friend M.E. Cadwallader. (364) Nettie's assertion corresponds with the historic record.

During this séance, Nettie, speaking for the spirits, lectured the President about the condition of the freed slaves. "While the spirits realized fully the many cares resting upon the President, there was duty to perform that could not be neglected—a duty that demanded immediate attention. They counseled him in the strongest terms to prove the truth of their statements, extravagant as they seemed, by appointing a special committee, whose duty it should be to investigate the condition of these people, and to receive their report in person, and on no account to receive it second hand," Nettie instructed. (365)

In her memoir it is clear that Nettie Colburn fully believed that the President took her message to heart. A few weeks later while visiting her parents in Hartford, New York, her father showed her a newspaper article reporting that President Lincoln was creating a commission to evaluate the condition of the freedmen. "This item confirmed what I had told my father more than a week before of my recent sitting at the White House. It also proved that Mr. Lincoln considered the counsel he had received through me sufficient importance to engage his attention, as he had literally followed the direction given him by the spirit world," Maynard crowed. (366)

The medium overestimated her influence with President Lincoln in this matter. Since the start of the war, the President had been aware of the plight of the freed slaves that flocked to contraband camps throughout the capital. Elizabeth Keckly, the First Lady's seamstress, had solicited the aide of the Lincolns in her fundraising efforts for the First Contraband Relief Society. (367) Throughout the war, Abraham and Mary Lincoln were frequent visitors to the contraband camps located outside of the Soldiers Home, where they passed out food from the White House kitchen and other sundry items desperately needed by the freedmen. (368)

It is highly likely, that the President was already in discussions about creating what became the Freedmen's Bureau well before Nettie relayed her spiritual message to the President. In actuality, if Nettie Colburn was telling the truth about the veracity of her message, what the medium actually did was provide reassurance to President Lincoln that he should pursue the establishment of the Freedmen's Bureau. Despite this moment of boasting, the medium's memoir is still a useful source for historians.

Nettie Colburn's memoir is a valuable source that sheds light into the career of a Spiritualist medium during the Civil War. Though she was unable to specify the exact number of séances preformed in the White House, her account testified that the President attended more séances than was previously been attributed by historians. According to Nettie in the introduction to her memoir, "Comparatively few of the *séances* with the President are given, as a number took place with Mrs. Lincoln alone as witness." (369)

As the strain of the Civil War began to emotionally and physically separate Abraham and Mary Lincoln, the couple's mutual interest in Spiritualism was one thing that kept them together. It is highly likely that Mary Lincoln scheduled a number these séances in a bid to spend time alone with her husband. "During the latter part of February, and the month of March [1864], I had a number of séances with President Lincoln and his wife; but, as there were no other witnesses, and as they did not inform me of the nature, but simply allude to the fact.

These séances took place by appointment. At the close of one, Mrs. Lincoln would make an appointment, engaging me to come at a certain hour of the day, which usually would be in the vicinity of one o'clock, the time when Mr. Lincoln usually partook of his luncheon, which generally occupied about half to three-quarters of an hour," Nettie disclosed. (370) Concerning the issues discussed during the séances, the medium would only admit, "Many subjects of interest were discussed at the various meetings I had with Mr. Lincoln." (371)

In one séance, Nettie illustrated her talent for military strategy. After becoming entranced, the medium awakened standing in front of a map of the Southern states with a pencil in her hand. "The only remarks I heard was these: 'It is astonishing,' said Mr. Lincoln, 'how every line she has drawn conforms to the plan agreed upon.' 'Yes,' answered the older soldier, 'it is very astonishing,'" Nettie Colburn claimed. (372) Upon leaving the President turned to the medium and reportedly said, "It is best not to mention this meeting at present." (373) Nettie promised that she would keep her consul about the events she had witnessed.

In her memoir, the medium used the events of that evening to conclude that President Lincoln shared his wife's interest in Spiritualism. "That it was important may be supposed, for those were not days for the indulgence of idle curiosity in any direction, nor was Mr. Lincoln a man to waste his time in giving exhibitions in occult science for the amusement of his friends," the medium concluded. (374) As 1864 drew to a close, the President had little time for recreation as he engaged in a hard fought campaign for re-election.

In November of 1864, President Lincoln was re-elected for a second term as President of the United States. The re-election campaign had been difficult as the President had to square off against the popular General George B. McClellan. (375) Despite the esteem the Union Army might have had for their "Little Mac," that esteem could not counter the love they had for their "Father Abraham," and the soldiers vote handily gave President Lincoln the election. (376)

Shortly after the election, President Lincoln received a congratulatory letter from the spirit of Edward D. Baker transmitted through a Spiritualist medium. Baker wanted to reassure his friend, "While your motives are pure and the spirits of the just—will hover around you and impress you of the right—Yes we saw you and witnessed your mind during the mighty struggle of the last political campaign—Your mind was calm and serene—You did not wish or pray that you might be reelected." (377)

If Lincoln had any doubts about God's support for the Union's war effort, Baker added, "You shall and will be directed by the Almighty ruler of all events." (378) After reassuring the President that victory was within reach, Baker then closed his letter with a request. "And now my dear friend I have a request to make of you—It is this—I want you to do us justice—by answering this and the receipt of the communication dated as follows March 23d 1862 November 14th 1862 November 29th 1864—I find the medium is honest and I want she should have the proof of the truthfulness of the spirits who have communicated through her to you— She being at the time in an unconscious state—I hope you will favor me by complying with this request—I know you will you are so kind." (379) The missives Baker mentioned in this letter have not survived. Though Lincoln failed to respond to this letter, he had a close relationship with his Washington, D.C. Spiritualist friends.

A curious event that occurred in December 1864 as related by Margaret Laurie to her friend William Chaney suggested that by the end of the Civil War the Lincolns had formed a unique relationship with their mediums. Chaney related the tale about the time that Margaret Laurie used her influence with the President to save the life of a soldier accused of desertion.

A young soldier from Maine was accused of desertion and sentenced to death after being apprehended in Boston with an expired furlough pass. According to the desperate soldier the sudden illness and death of his sister had kept him from returning to his post on time. (380) A friend of the condemned soldier rushed to Washington, D.C. to seek a pardon from President Lincoln. Unfortunately, the young man arrived at the White House after the President had retired for bed with orders that he was not to be disturbed. (381)

Deaf to his pleading, the sergeant on duty refused to admit the soldier's friend. "But the sergeant softened enough to tell him that he had orders to admit Mrs. Laurie at any hour, day or night," Chaney recorded in 1886. Rushing to Margaret Laurie's home the young man explained his plight and enlisted the medium in his cause. Moved by the young man's story, according to Chaney, the medium "hurried to the White House, reprieve in hand, and was instantly admitted to the room where the President and his wife were asleep. Mr. Lincoln aroused himself with great difficulty. In a few words she explained her mission, which he seemed to understand intuitively more than by his consciousness. Without speaking he motioned her to hand him a pen from the table, and as he put his name to the reprieve, with a moistened eye and trembling lip, he said: 'Thank you, Mrs. Laurie; never fear to arouse me on an errand of mercy like this.'" (382)

Unlike most of the stories related by the Spiritualist who associated with the Lincolns, this one can be verified. The collection of Lincoln papers that are presently housed in the Library of Congress contains a letter written on December 19, 1864 from a Mrs. M.A. Laurie to President Lincoln requesting a pardon for Elbert F. Turner. "Will the President have the kindness to pardon...if I beg he will for the sake of suffering humanity, and I believe justice, release Elbert F. Turner today," M.A. Laurie begged the President. (383) The events recorded by William Chaney and the name on the letter are too similar to be a coincidence. It appears that the Mrs. M.A. Laurie in the letter was in fact the Spiritualist medium Margaret Laurie.

The burdens of the war weighed heavily on the President. As the incident with Margaret Laurie illustrated, it became increasingly difficult for President Abraham Lincoln to receive a peaceful night's slumber. During the winter of 1864-1865, Nettie attended the weekly receptions hosted by Mary Lincoln on Tuesday afternoons. This allowed the medium to personally witness the strain the Civil War had placed on President Lincoln.

"He never seemed to have an idle moment, nor did he ever appear to relax his manner of reserve, nor give way to excessive mirthfulness, even at a time when witty sayings were a part of the conversation," Nettie sadly remembered. (384) Only through Spiritualist séances did the President receive any form of comfort, according to Nettie. "It should be borne in mind that all my meetings with Mr. Lincoln were periods of special import, and upon occasions when he was in need of aid and direction. After the 'circle,' which he attended, he invariably left with a brighter and happier look, evidencing the benefit in part which he experienced from that which had been imparted to him," Nettie insisted. (385)

The Lincolns' interest in Spiritualism proved to be more than a passing fad following Willie's death. After being introduced to Spiritualism by his wife, President Lincoln continued to regular attend séances in the White House and at the Laurie's Georgetown residence. Though the President was a regular fixture at his wife's séances, President Lincoln's position on the religion remained frustratingly unclear. While he was recorded by Spiritualists as saying that he was intrigued by some of the phenomena that he witnessed, his exact feelings on the religion remain unknown.

As word spread of President Lincoln's involvement in Spiritualism, the President received harsh criticism. On the eve of a highly contested re-election campaign, the President wisely decided to remain discreet on the issue. While the ranks of Spiritualists had grown with the slaughter produced by the Civil War, the religion was still controversial. Instead of distancing himself from Spiritualism, President Lincoln just kept his movement within the Spiritualist community discreet. Despite having been targeted by a fraudulent medium, Abraham and Mary Lincoln continued to attend séances conducted by their favorite medium Nettie Colburn. All this illustrated that President Abraham Lincoln shared his wife's interest in Spiritualism.

Conclusion

"I shall live till my work is done"

On Friday April 14, 1865, President Abraham Lincoln held a Cabinet meeting to discuss the beginning of Reconstruction. The President was in a good mood. The surrender of General Robert E. Lee's Confederate army had ended the fighting in Virginia. All that was needed to cement the Union victory was word from General William Tecumseh Sherman in North Carolina that Confederate General Joseph E. Johnston had surrendered his forces.

This news President Lincoln believed would be shortly received because the night before he had had a dream. Secretary of the Navy Gideon Welles, curious about the nature of the dream asked the President to explain his statement. "He said it related to your (my) element, the water; that he seemed to be in some singular, indescribable vessel, and that he was moving with great rapidity towards an indefinite shore; that he had this dream preceding Sumter, Bull Run, Antietam, Gettysburg, Stone River, Vicksburg, Wilmington, etc.," Welles recorded in his diary. (386)

When General Ulysses S. Grant interjected that the Battle of Stone's River was not a Union Victory and that nothing good had come out of it, the President remained nonplussed. "I had," Lincoln continued, "this strange dream again last night, and we shall, judging from the past, have great news very soon. I think it must be from Sherman. My thoughts are in that direction, as are most of yours." (387) As the day wore on, it became apparent that President Abraham Lincoln's dream was indeed prophetic, but not in the way the President had expected.

"I write this conversation three days after it occurred in consequence of what took place Friday night, and but for which the mention of this dream would probably have never been noted. Great events did, indeed, follow, for within a few hours the good and gentle, as well as truly great, man who narrated his dream closed forever his earthly career," Gideon Welles sadly noted in his diary. (388)

As the Civil War drew to the close, Nettie Colburn asserted in her memoir that she tried to warn the President that his life was in danger. (389) During her last audience with Abraham Lincoln in February 1865 the medium again tried to voice her concern. Nettie Colburn and her friend Parthia Hannum came to the White House to express their regret that they could not attend the inauguration as Nettie had just received word that her father was seriously ill. (390) After some pleasant small talk, the President asked Nettie, "But what do our friends say of us now?" To which the medium replied, "What they predicted for you, Mr. Lincoln, has come to pass, and you are to be inaugurated the second time." (391)

To this statement Lincoln nodded his head, Nettie then tried to warn the President, "But they also re-affirm that the shadow they have spoken of still hangs over you." President Lincoln did not wish to speak about his safety with the spirits as Nettie recalled his reaction, "He turned half impatiently away and said, 'Yes, I know. I have letters from all over the country from your kind of people—mediums, I mean—warning me against some dreadful plot against my life. But I don't think the knife is made, or the bullet run, that will reach it. Besides, nobody wants to harm me,'" Nettie recalled Lincoln saying. The President then tried to soothe the medium, "Well, Miss Nettie, I shall live till my work is done, and no earthly power can prevent it. And then it doesn't matter so that I am ready—and that I ever mean to be." (392)

As time wore on President Abraham Lincoln received more warnings that his time on earth was drawing to a close. A few weeks before his death, legend holds that the President dreamed of his own death. Like he had with his election night vision in 1860, Lincoln confided to Mary the nature of the dream:

"About ten days ago…I retired very late. I had been waiting for important dispatches from the front. I could not have been long in bed when I fell into a slumber, for I was weary. I soon began to dream.

There seemed to be a death-like stillness about me. Then I heard subdued sobs, as if a number of people were weeping. I thought I left my bed and wandered downstairs. There the silence was broken by the same pitiful sobbing, but the mourners were invisible.

I went from room to room; no living person was in sight, but the same mournful sounds of distress met me as I passed along. It was light in all the rooms; every object was familiar to me; but where were all the people who were grieving as if their hearts would break? I was puzzled and alarmed. What could be the meaning of all this?

Determined to find the cause of a state of things so mysterious and so shocking, I kept on until I arrived at the East Room, which I entered. There I met with a sickening surprise. Before me was a catafalque, on which rested a corpse wrapped in funeral vestments. Around it were stationed soldiers who were acting as guards; and there was a throng of people, some gazing mournfully upon the corpse, whose face was covered, others weeping pitifully.

'Who is dead in the White House?' I demanded of one of the soldiers.

'The President,' was his answer; 'He was killed by an assassin!'

Then came a loud burst of grief from the crowd, which awoke me from my dream. I slept no more that night; and although it was only a dream, I have been strangely annoyed by it ever since." (393)

Unbeknownst to the President, John Wilkes Booth, an ardent Southern sympathizer, plotted President Lincoln's death. Swelled by grief and racism, Booth sought the ultimate act of revenge against the man he blamed for the Civil War and the destruction of his beloved South. Perhaps President Lincoln did have some notion that his time had come. On Good Friday, April 14, 1865, the President remarked to his cabinet that he had the night before the dream that he always had before momentous events.

Later that night, the President turned to White House guard William H. Crook and made a passing remark that would stay with the man for the rest of his life. "When he was about to enter the White House he said 'Good-bye,' as I never remember to have heard him say before when I was leaving for the night," Crook recalled in his memoir. "These things have a curious interest. President Lincoln was a man of entire sanity. But no one has ever sounded the spring of spiritual insight from which his nature fed. To me it all means that he had, with his waking that day, a strong prescience of coming change," Crook concluded. (394)

A few hours later, John Wilkes Booth assassinated President Abraham Lincoln at Ford's Theatre while the Lincolns were enjoying the comedy *Our American Cousins*. Too weak to be moved to the White House, the President was moved to the Petersons Boarding House located across the street from the theatre. There President Abraham Lincoln died at 7:22 A.M. surrounded by his cabinet officers and his son Robert. Mary Lincoln was not in the room, she had been banished from her husband's bedside by Secretary of War Edwin Stanton because her crying annoyed him. (395)

After the President's death, Mary Lincoln returned to the White House to grieve. Though she refused to see many of the guests who came to offer her their sympathies, the First Lady welcomed her Spiritualist friends. At the time of the President's death Nettie Colburn was not in the city, and she never saw any of the Lincolns' again.

While Nettie could not come to the White House, two female Spiritualists did come. "Mrs. Lincoln was almost frantic with suffering. Women spiritualists in some way gained access to her. They poured into her ears pretended messages from her dead husband. Mrs. Lincoln was so weakened that she had not force enough to resist the cruel cheat. These women nearly crazed her. Mr. Robert Lincoln, who had to take his place now at the head of the family, finally ordered them out of the house," White House guard William Crook recalled. (396) Though it is impossible to verify the identity of the two Spiritualists, it is likely that the women mentioned were Margaret Laurie and her daughter Belle Miller.

After her husband's death, Mary Lincoln lost her anchor in life. Too grief stricken to return to her Springfield home, Mary moved to Chicago with Robert and Tad. During the first years of her widowhood, Mary stopped meeting with mediums and attending séances writing in 1867, "I am not EITHER a spiritualist—but I sincerely believe—our loved ones, who have only, 'gone before' are permitted to watch over those who were dearer to them than life." (397) Instead of attending séances, Mary Lincoln turned to Spiritualist literature and a sojourn in Europe in an attempt to find some solace. Following the Civil War Spiritualism reached new audiences through Elizabeth Stuart Phelps's widely popular novel *The Gates Ajar*.

Published in 1868, the novel chronicles the orphaned Mary Cabot's diary entries that testified to her intense grief following the death of her brother Roy in the Civil War. Through the ministrations of her Aunt Winifred, Mary comes to terms with the loss of her brother by the assurance that Roy is not just a distant angel in heaven, but "close to me; somehow or other to be near as—to be nearer than—he was here—*really mine again.*" (398)

Like countless grieving Americans, Mary Lincoln turned to *The Gates Ajar* for comfort. (399) One particular passage must have brought the grieving widow immeasurable comfort as it dealt with her personal loss. "I wonder if Roy has seen the President [in heaven]. Aunt Winifred says she does not doubt it. She thinks that all the soldiers must have crowded up to meet him, and 'O,' she says, 'what a sight to see!'" the fictional Mary Cabot writes. (400) The novel had a tremendous emotional reaction for Mary. While residing in England, Mary Lincoln wrote to her friend Eliza Slataper advising her to read the novel. "I have been reading, a little book—which made me think much of you. It is called, 'Gates Ajar,' by Mrs. Phillips do get it & read it—it is by an American lady, & has created quite a sensation in Europe, this Autumn," Mary wrote. (401) Sadly as events would unfold, Mary Lincoln would need the spiritual comfort provided by *The Gates Ajar* and other publications.

Dissatisfied and lonely in Europe, Mary and Tad Lincoln returned to Chicago in the summer of 1871. During the journey home Tad became ill, back in Chicago his condition continued to deteriorate and on July 15, 1871, the eighteen-year-old died. Following Tad's death, Mary Lincoln became actively involved in Spiritualism again. (402) A year after Tad's death Mary Lincoln visited the studio of the notorious spirit photographer William H. Mumler. The Boston photographer had gained notoriety in press during the 1860's for his spirit photographs. (403) Tried for fraud in New York in 1869, Mumler had beaten the charges and had returned to his native Boston. (404) According to Mumler, the former First Lady visited his studio and gave her name as Mrs. Lindall. (405) Swathed in black, the photographer claimed that he did not recognize Mary Lincoln.

A few days later, Mary returned to the studio to pick up her photograph. When another customer turned to Mary and asked her if she recognized the spirit in the image, Mrs. Mumler who claimed to be a medium became entranced by the spirit of Tad. Turning to Mary, Mrs. Mumler declared, "Mother, if you cannot recognize father, show the picture to Robert; he will recognize it." (406)

Shocked by Mrs. Mumler's statement, Mary Lincoln revealed her true identity and continued to converse with the medium. According to William H. Mumler, "When my wife resumed her normal condition, she found Mrs. L. weeping tears of joy that she had again found her loved ones, and apparently anxious to learn, if possible, how long before she could join them in their spirit home. But this information of course could not be given." (407) The last photograph to be taken of Mary Lincoln showed a woman aged by grief with the ghostly image of her husband resting his hands on her shoulders with the shadow outline of Tad standing behind his mother.

In the spring of 1875, Mary Lincoln suffered a mental collapse that was likely triggered by the 10th anniversary of her husband's death. (408) Robert Lincoln, embarrassed and worried about his mother had her committed to Bellevue Place Sanitarium in Batavia, Illinois. (409) Released after a short stay in the institution, Mary Lincoln continued to live a vagabond life in Europe until her health forced her to return to Springfield, Illinois. There in the house of her sister Elizabeth Edwards, Mary Lincoln passed away on July 16, 1882. (410)

Following President Abraham Lincoln's death, Spiritualists latched onto his memory proclaiming that the late President was a devout Spiritualist. Following the death and carnage of the Civil War the Spiritualist ranks swelled with grieving parents and widows. In 1888, J. B. McClure reprinted a number of anecdotes and stories about President Abraham Lincoln copied from an 1864 tract entitled *Old Abe's Joke Book*. Included in the volume was a reprint of the *Boston Evening Gazette* story written by Prior Melton about Charles E. Shockle's White House spirit circle under the heading "A Curious Story of Lincoln and the Spirits—A 'Séance.'" (411) For Spiritualists, this proved conformation that President Lincoln belonged to the faith.

Further supporting Spiritualist claims were the articles written by Jack Laurie and W.H. Chaney that were published in the Spiritualist publication *The Religio-Philosophical Journal*. The allegation that President Abraham Lincoln was a Spiritualist angered some of the President's associates. "Mr. Lincoln was greatly annoyed by the report that he was interested in spiritualism," President Lincoln's pastor the Reverend Dr. Phineas Gurley declared. (412)

Despite their prostrations, the memoirs continued to be published. Nettie Colburn Maynard asserted that the purpose behind her memoir was to record a significant moment in American history. Others used their stories to spread Spiritualism. As Colonel Simon Kase proclaimed in his memoir, "Having given somewhat in detail the facts and circumstances attending the investigation of modern Spiritualism by President Lincoln, and the results brought about by angelic or supernatural influence, and my connection with it, let me indulge the hope that the reader will seek the truth by such fair and honest investigation as may be thought necessary for a realization of the wonderful phenomena, which was instrumental in relieving at one stroke of the pen the heavy weight that pressed four millions of human beings down under the barbarous power of slavery." (413)

President Abraham Lincoln remained a fixture within the Spiritualist community well into the turn of the century. During a Spiritualist convention in 1909 held in St. Joseph, Missouri one delegate proclaimed, "Lincoln was the first Spiritualist of any consequence in this country." (414) Countering this statement another delegate, Reverend Thomas Grimshaw, asserted that "It would hardly be fair to designate Lincoln as a Spiritualist, though he is known to have accepted in a general way the truths of our religion." (415)

After World War I, interest in Spiritualism dwindled. By the 1960's, Spiritualism had been incorporated into the New Age movement. Following this transition, Abraham and Mary Lincolns' metaphysical beliefs became the fodder of paranormal investigators. Writers Christopher Coleman, Susan B. Martinez, and Troy Taylor focused on the dreams and visions the President experienced as evidence that the Lincolns had encountered the paranormal. The stories that President Lincoln's ghost's is haunting the White House have become a staple of the literature on America's ghosts and mysteries. (416)

Following on this trend, Mary Lincoln's belief in Spiritualism has also entered popular culture. In movies, plays, and television shows, popular culture has reinforced the notion that only Mary Lincoln was interested in Spiritualism during the Civil War. The best example of this portrayal is featured in the 1988 mini-series *Gore Vidal's Lincoln*, where Abraham Lincoln played by Sam Waterston walks into a séance being held for Mary Lincoln played by Mary Tyler Moore. Obviously dismayed with his wife's activities, Lincoln has no interest in the séance and playfully chides Mary until an aide interrupts and calls Lincoln away. (417) In the play *The Heavens Are Hung in Black*, Lincoln retreats to his office during a séance where he complains about his wife's belief in Spiritualism to his secretary John Hay. "Not even a single babel of incoherence as far as I could tell. Oh, someone coughed once and the entire mess of them mistook it for a visit from Lord Bryon. It's queer with those types: they're interested in what you have to say only if you're dead. The entire exhibition made me want to hang myself so I took leave before I expired and became a visiting spirit myself. I find the theatre far more entertaining than the occult—even though the two somehow hide behind the same family tree," playwright James Still has Lincoln declare. (418)

Mary Lincoln's belief in Spiritualism has also been used in comedy as historical jokes about the First Lady's alleged mental instability. In the 2000 made for TV movie, actress Shirley MacLaine parodied her well known interest in metaphysics when her character a former Hollywood starlet declares to her son, "You did not have a job for me when you were making that Mary Todd Lincoln show. And you knew that I wanted to play Mary Todd Lincoln! I see spirits too!" (419)

Even in shows meant to appeal to a younger, hipper audience, references to Mary Lincoln's belief in Spiritualism has been featured in the Fox TV animated series *American Dad*. In the third season episode "Black Mystery Month" which parodies the novel and movie *The Da Vinci Code* and Black History Month writer Laura McCreary featured the main characters CIA agent Stan Smith and his son Steve on a madcap adventure to discover the truth about the invention of peanut butter. After narrowly escaping death, Stan admits the hidden truth, that peanut butter was actually invented by Mary Lincoln in an attempt to ward off evil spirits. As President Lincoln informs William Seward and Simon Chase, "Don't eat that! That's one of my wife's lunatic concoctions for staving off evil spirits!" The camera then pans over to Mary Lincoln is standing in the cornering murmuring about man someday waling on the moon while playing with a paddle ball. (420) As these brief examples have shown, Mary Lincoln's belief in Spiritualism have captured the imagination of the American public for generations, yet President Lincoln's involvement in Spiritualism has continued to be neglected—until now.

Evidence shows that throughout their lives Abraham and Mary Lincoln shared an interest in metaphysical beliefs. Abraham and Mary Lincoln were born into a culture that intertwined metaphysical beliefs with Christianity. The Lincolns' beliefs were a product of their culture and upbringing. During his life, long before he became President, Abraham Lincoln expressed his belief in dreams. Lincoln had dreams and visions which he perceived as being prophetic in nature. Abraham and Mary Lincoln even used metaphysics to heal the physical body when traditional medicine had failed to produce the desired results.

President Abraham Lincoln shared his wife's interest in Spiritualism during the dark days of the Civil War. Like countless America's, the
Lincolns' retreated to the darkened séance chamber in an attempt to encounter the divine and to gather clarity and insight into the momentous
events they faced. That Abraham and Mary Lincoln attended Spiritualist
séances while in the White House should not be a surprise when viewed
within the context of their lifelong metaphysical beliefs. The Lincolns'
where a product of their culture, both where born into communities that
relied on metaphysical practices, Abraham and Mary Lincoln came to
maturity believing in the power of dreams and visions. In this aspect the
Lincolns' were not unique. Following the deaths of two beloved sons
and the carnage of the Civil War, the Lincolns turned to Spiritualism to
assuage their grief. Again, in this aspect the Lincolns' were not the only
couple that turned to Spiritualism during the Civil War.

What made the Lincolns' interest in Spiritualism unique was that
Abraham Lincoln was President of the United States. Even their critics
during the war did not have a problem with Spiritualism per se, but with
the President's attendance at séances in the White House. That the Lincolns' held Spiritualist séances in the White House has dismayed generations of Lincoln scholars who have tried to minimize the President's interest in Spiritualism by placing the blame on Mary Lincoln.

For decades historians have maintained that President Lincoln only attended one or two séances in an attempt to protect his mentally unstable wife. This is simply not the case as the primary sources show that President Abraham Lincoln attended likely a dozen séances during the Civil War. During these séances, the President was an enthusiastic participant, actively engaging with the mediums and the spirits. Based on the evidence presented Spiritualism played a significant, if not critical, role in Abraham Lincoln's White House—a fact that has been ignored by historians for a 150 years.

CITATIONS

1. Christopher Kiernan Coleman, *The Paranormal Presidency of Abraham Lincoln* (Atglen: Schiffer Publishing, Ltd., 2012), 86.

2. Coleman, *The Paranormal Presidency of Abraham Lincoln*, 86.

3. William H. Herndon, "Letters from Lincoln's Old Partner," *Religio-Philosophical Journal*, December 12, 1885 (Courtesy of the Peabody Room, District of Columbia Public Library, Georgetown Neighborhood Branch).

4. Stephen Mansfield, *Lincoln's Battle with God: A President's Struggle with Faith and What it Meant for America* (Nashville: Thomas Nelson, 2012), 161-162.

5. Catherine L. Albanese, *A Republic of Mind & Spirit: A Cultural History of American Metaphysical Religion* (New Haven: Yale University Press, 2007), 66.

6. Albanese, *A Republic of Mind & Spirit*, 6.

7. Jason Emerson, *The Madness of Mary Lincoln* (Carbondale: Southern Illinois University Press, 2007), 33.

8. David Herbert Donald, *Lincoln at Home: Two Glimpses of Abraham Lincoln's Domestic Life* (Washington, D.C.: White House Historical Association, 1999), 27.

9. Mansfield, *Lincoln's Battle with God*, 155.

10. Mansfield, *Lincoln's Battle with God*, 155.

11. Irving Stone, "Mary Todd Lincoln: A Final Judgment?" (Springfield: Abraham Lincoln Association, 1973), 7.

12. Jay Monaghan, "Was Abraham Lincoln Really a Spiritualist?" *Journal of the Illinois State Historical Society*, vol. 34, no. 2 (June 1941): 209.

13. Jean H. Baker, *Mary Todd Lincoln* (New York: W.W. Norton and Company, 1987), 206. For more on the numerous transformation's the White House has undergone over two hundred years see Vicki Goldberg, *The White House: The President's Home in Photographs and History* (New York: Little, Brown and Company, 2011).

14. Elizabeth Keckley, *Behind the Scenes: Formerly a Slave, But More Recently Modiste, and Friend to Mrs. Lincoln Or, Thirty Years a Slave and Four Years in the White House* (Chicago: The Lakeside Press, 1998), 83.

15. Keckley, *Behind the Scenes*, 84.

16. Keckley, *Behind the Scenes*, 83.

17. Historian Jennifer Fleischner through an examination of Elizabeth Keckly's signature proved that Keckly did not spell her name as "Keckley." Jennifer Fleischner, *Mrs. Lincoln and Mrs. Keckly: The Remarkable Story of the Friendship between a First Lady and a Former Slave* (New York: Broadway Books, 2003). Note: in the notes I use the spelling "Keckley" as it was spelled by the publisher of Elizabeth Keckly's memoir.

18. Keckley, *Behind the Scenes*, 84.

19. Mansfield, *Lincoln's Battle with God*, 136.

20. Keckley, *Behind the Scenes,* 82.

21. Catherine Clinton, *Mrs. Lincoln: A Life* (New York: Harper, 2009), 167.

22. Keckley, *Behind the Scenes*, 88.

23. Merrill D. Peterson, *Lincoln in American Memory* (New York: Oxford University Press, 1994), 262, 328.

24. See Baker, *Mary Todd Lincoln*, 221. Clinton, *Mrs. Lincoln*, 187. Doris Kearns Goodwin, *Team of Rivals: The Political Genius of Abraham Lincoln* (New York: Simon and Shuster, 2005), 509.

25. Benjamin P. Thomas, *Abraham Lincoln: A Biography* (New York: The Modern Library, 1952, 1968), 4.

26. Mansfield, *Lincoln's Battle with God*, 23. David Herbert Donald, *Lincoln* (New York: Simon & Schuster, 1995), 24.

27. Mansfield, *Lincoln's Battle with God*, xvii.

28. Albanese, *A Republic of Mind and Spirit*, 21-22.

29. Coleman, *The Paranormal Presidency of Abraham Lincoln* , 11.

30. Mansfield, *Lincoln's Battle with God*, 121.

31. Thomas, *Abraham Lincoln*, 8.

32. Mansfield, *Lincoln's Battle with God*, 23.

33. Richard Campanella, *Lincoln in New Orleans: The 1828-1831 Flatboat Voyages and Their Place in History* (Lafayette: University of Louisiana at Lafayette Press, 2010), 32-33.

34. Campanella, *Lincoln in New Orleans*, 143

35. Campanella, *Lincoln in New Orleans*, 212.

36. Susan B. Martinez, *The Psychic Life of Abraham Lincoln* (Franklin Lakes: New Page Books, 2009), 27.

37. Coleman, *The Paranormal Presidency of Abraham Lincoln*, 25.

38. Campanella, *Lincoln in New Orleans,* 212.

39. Mansfield, *Lincoln's Battle with God*, 31.

40. Mansfield, *Lincoln's Battle with God*, 42-43.

41. For more on the background on New Salem's residents see Benjamin P. Thomas, *Lincoln's New Salem* (Carbondale: Southern Illinois University Press, 1954, 1988).

42. Thomas, *Lincoln's New Salem*, 60. Coleman, *The Paranormal Presidency of Abraham Lincoln*, 11.

43. Wayne C. Temple, *Abraham Lincoln: From Skeptic to Prophet* (Mahomet: Mayhaven Publishing, 1995), 17.

44. Baker, *Mary Todd Lincoln*, 17.

45. Baker, *Mary Todd Lincoln*, 19.

46. Clinton, *Mrs. Lincoln*, 338. Paul E. Johnson and Sean Wilentz, *The Kingdom of Matthias: A Story of Sex and Salvation in 19th-Century America* (Oxford: Oxford University Press, 1994), 50.

47. Clinton, *Mrs. Lincoln*, 12.

48. Fleischner, *Mrs. Lincoln and Mrs. Keckly*, 48.

49. Fleischner, *Mrs. Lincoln and Mrs. Keckly*, 48.

50. Kenneth J. Winkle, *Abraham and Mary Lincoln* (Carbondale: Southern Illinois University Press, 2011), 17.

51. Clinton, *Mrs. Lincoln*, 12.

52. See Albert J. Raboteau, *Slave Religion: The "Invisible Institution" in the Antebellum South* (Oxford: Oxford University Press, 2004).

53. Katherine Helm, *The True Story of Mary, Wife of Lincoln: Containing the Recollections of Mary Lincoln's Sister Emilie (Mrs. Ben Hardin Helm), Extracts from Her War-Time Diary, Numerous Letters and Other Documents now First published* (New York: Harper and Brothers Publishing, 1928), 23-24.

54. Helm, *True Story of Mary*, 24.

55. Helm, *True Story of Mary*, 25.

56. Carol Berkin, *Civil War Wives: The Lives & Times of Angelina Grimké Weld, Varina Howell Davis & Julia Dent Grant* (New York: Alfred A. Knopf, 2009), 229.

57. Clinton, *Mrs. Lincoln*, 26.

58. Clinton, *Mrs. Lincoln*, 26.

59. Clinton, *Mrs. Lincoln*, 25.

60. Baker, *Mary Todd Lincoln*, 75.

61. Daniel Mark Epstein, *The Lincolns: Portrait of a Marriage* (New York: Ballantine Books, 2008), 49.

62. Clinton, *Mrs. Lincoln*, 14.

63. Epstein, *The Lincolns*, 50.

64. Barbara Weisberg, *Talking to the Dead: Katie and Maggie Fox and the Rise of Spiritualism* (San Francisco: HarperSanFrancisco, 2004), 1-2.

65. Weisberg, *Talking to the Dead*, 4.

66. Weisberg, *Talking to the Dead*, 4.

67. Clinton, *Mrs. Lincoln*, 186.

68. Emily Alter, "The Spiritualist Movement and its Advancement of the Nineteenth Century Women's Movement," *The Concord Review*, (2001), 172.

69. Emma Hardinge, *Modern American Spiritualism: A Twenty Years' Record of the Communion between Earth and the World of the Spirits* (New York: Emma Hardinge, 1870), 72.

70. Geoffrey K. Nelson, *Spiritualism and Society* (New York: Schocken Books, 1969), 5.

71. Alter, "The Spiritualist Movement and its Advancement of the Nineteenth Century Women's Movement," 174.

72. See Ann Braude, *Radical Spirits: Spiritualism and Women's Rights in Nineteenth-Century America* (Bloomington: Indiana University Press, 1989, 2001).

73. Catherine Allgor, *Parlor Politics: In Which the Ladies of Washington Build a City and a Government* (Charlottesville: University of Virginia Press, 2000), 76-77.

74. Drew Gilpin Faust, *This Republic of Suffering: Death and the American Civil War* (New York: Alfred A. Knopf, 2008), 181.

75. David S. Reynolds, *Mightier than the Sword: Uncle Tom's Cabin and the Battle for America* (New York: W.W. Norton & Company, 2011), 46

76. Faust, *This Republic of Suffering*, 181.

77. Faust, *This Republic of Suffering*, 181.

78. E.W. Capron, *Modern Spiritualism its Facts and Fanaticisms its Consistencies and Contradictions* (Boston: Bela Marsh, 1855), 355.

79. Michael F. Holt, *Franklin Pierce* (New York: Times Books, 2010), 18, 28.

80. Holt, *Franklin Pierce*, 50.

81. Dwight Young and Margaret Johnson, *Dear First Lady: Letters to the White House from the Collections of the Library of Congress and National Archives* (Washington, D.C.: National Geographic, 2008), 33.

82. Young and Johnson, *Dear First Lady*, 34.

83. Weisberg, *Talking to the Dead*, 162.

84. Julia Taft Bayne, *Tad's Lincoln's Father* (Lincoln: University of Nebraska Press, 2001), 74-75.

85. Coleman, *The Paranormal Presidency of Abraham Lincoln*, 17.

86. Joe Nickell, "Paranormal Lincoln," *Skeptical Inquirer*, vol. 23 (May/June 1999), accessed January 31, 2013 http://www.csicop.org/si/show/paranormal-_lincoln/.

87. Epstein, *The Lincolns*, 77-78.

88. Weisberg, *Talking to the Dead*, 25.

89. Weisberg, *Talking to the Dead*, 26.

90. Weisberg, *Talking to the Dead*, 25.

91. Weisberg, *Talking to the Dead*, 26.

92. Cox, *Body and Soul*, 41-42.

93. Clinton, *Mrs. Lincoln*, 183.

94. Epstein, *The Lincolns*, 78.

95. Robert Todd Lincoln was born on August 1, 1843 and was followed by Edward "Eddie" Baker Lincoln who was born on March 10, 1846.

96. David Herbert Donald, *Lincoln at Home: Two Glimpses of Abraham Lincoln's Domestic Life* (Washington, D.C.: White House Historical Association, 1999), 48-49.

97. Coleman, *The Paranormal Presidency of Abraham Lincoln*, 145.

98. Coleman, *The Paranormal Presidency of Abraham Lincoln*, 12.

99. Martinez, *The Psychic Life of Abraham Lincoln*, 92.

100. Baker, *Mary Todd Lincoln*, 126-128.

101. Clinton, *Mrs. Lincoln*, 86.

102. Baker, *Mary Todd Lincoln*, 126.

103. Jason Emerson, *The Madness of Mary Lincoln* (Carbondale: Southern Illinois University, 2007), 12.

104. Clinton, *Mrs. Lincoln*, 87.

105. Clinton, *Mrs. Lincoln*, 87.

106. Baker, *Mary Todd Lincoln*, 127.

107. "But Jesus said, Suffer little children, and forbid them not, to come unto me: for such is the kingdom of Heaven"—Matthew 19:14 (King James Bible). The headstone is now on display at the Abraham Lincoln Presidential Museum in Springfield, Illinois.

108. Baker, *Mary Todd Lincoln*, 127.

109. Mansfield, *Lincoln's Battle with God*, 86.

110. *Daily Illinois State Journal*, June 19, 1851, 2. (Courtesy of the Sangamon Valley Collection, Lincoln Library, Springfield, IL).

111. *Daily Illinois State Journal*, March 3, 1858, 3. (Courtesy of the Sangamon Valley Collection, Lincoln Library, Springfield, IL).

112. *Daily Illinois State Journal*, October 20, 1858, 2. (Courtesy of the Sangamon Valley Collection, Lincoln Library, Springfield, IL).

113. *Daily Illinois State Journal*, November 17, 1858, 3. *Daily Illinois State Journal*, November 18, 1858, 3. (Courtesy of the Sangamon Valley Collection, Lincoln Library, Springfield, IL).

114. *Daily Illinois State Journal*, December 21, 1858, 3. (Courtesy of the Sangamon Valley Collection, Lincoln Library, Springfield, IL).

115. Braude, *Radical Spirits*, 104-105.

116. *Daily Illinois State Journal*, December 15, 1859, 3. (Courtesy of the Sangamon Valley Collection, Lincoln Library, Springfield, IL). For more on the fascinating life of Achsa W. Sprague see Ann Braude's *Radical Spirits.*

117. William H. Herndon, "Letters from Lincoln's Old Partner," *Religio-Philosophical Journal*, December 12, 1885 (Courtesy of the Peabody Room, District of Columbia Public Library, Georgetown Neighborhood Branch).

118. Wayne C. Temple, "Herndon on Lincoln: An Unknown Interview with a List of Books in the Lincoln & Herndon Law Office," *Journal of the Illinois State Historical Society* (vol. 98, no. 1/2), 38.

119. Temple, "Herndon on Lincoln," 38, 39, 45.

120. Temple, "Herndon on Lincoln," 38.

121. Justin G. Turner and Linda Levitt Turner, *Mary Todd Lincoln: Her Life and Letters* (New York: Alfred A. Knopf, 1972), 607.

122. Troy Taylor, *The Haunted President: The History, Hauntings & Supernatural Life of Abraham Lincoln* (Decatur: Whitechapel Press, 2005, 2009), 58.

123. Taylor, *The Haunted President*, 58.

124. Sandra Brue, Mike Capps, and Timothy P. Townsend, *Abraham Lincoln: A Living Legacy: A Guide to Three Abraham Lincoln National Park Sites* (Virginia Beach: The Donning Company Publishers, 2008), 135.

125. Bruce Chadwick, *Lincoln for President: An Unlikely Candidate, an Audacious Strategy, and the Victory No One Saw Coming* (Naperville: Sourcebooks, Inc., 2009), 301.

126. Brue, Capps, and Townsend, *Abraham Lincoln*, 135.

127. Baker, *Mary Todd Lincoln*, 162.

128. Like nearly every incident in the life of Abraham and Mary Lincoln there are two versions of how Abraham gave Mary the good news following his election. I have based my interpretation by blending the two stories. For the version that has Mary Lincoln asleep in bed see Chadwick *Lincoln for President*, 308. Abraham Lincoln's statement to his wife is featured in Jean H. Baker's *Mary Todd Lincoln*, 161-162.

129. Noah Brooks, "Recollections of Abraham Lincoln," *Harper's New Monthly Magazine* (July 1865): 224.

130. Brooks, "Recollections of Abraham Lincoln," 224-225.

131. Brooks, "Recollections of Abraham Lincoln," 225.

132. Brooks, "Recollections of Abraham Lincoln," 225.

133. Brooks, "Recollections of Abraham Lincoln," 225.

134. Coleman, *The Paranormal Presidency of Abraham Lincoln*, 77.

135. Harold Holzer, *Lincoln President-Elect: Abraham Lincoln and the Great Secession Winter 1860-1861* (New York: Simon & Schuster, 2008), 5.

136. Lloyd Ostendorf, *The Photographs of Mary Todd Lincoln* (Springfield: Illinois State Historical Society, 1969), 4.

137. Clinton, *Mrs. Lincoln*, 120.

138. Baker, *Mary Todd Lincoln*, 164.

139. Daniel Stashower, *The Hour of Peril: The Secret Plot to Murder Lincoln before the Civil War* (New York: Minotaur Books, 2013), 83.

140. Thomas Richmond, *God Dealing With Slavery* (Chicago: Religio-Philosophical Publishing House, 1870), 73-74.

141. Richmond, *God Dealing With Slavery*, 74.

142. James Marten, *Children for the Union: The War Spirit on the Northern Home Front* (Chicago: Ivan R. Dee, 2004), 25-26.

143. "G.A. A Wide Awake to Abraham Lincoln, Tuesday, December 11, 1860," Abraham Lincoln Papers at the Library of Congress, accessed November 3, 2011, http://memory.loc.gov/cgi-bin/query/r?ammem/mal:@field(DOCID+lit (do497700)).

144. "G.A. A Wide Awake to Abraham Lincoln."

145. Faust, *This Republic of Suffering*, 181.

146. William J. Cooper, *We Have the War upon Us: The Onset of the Civil War, November 1860-April 1861* (New York: Alfred A. Knopf, 2012), 9.

147. "The President Elect A Spiritualist," *The Waukesha Freeman*, March 12, 1861, 1, 3.

148. "The President Elect A Spiritualist," 3.

149. "The President Elect A Spiritualist," 3.

150. "Astrological Predictions: The Presidential Campaign of 1860," *Lincoln Lore*, 1433 (July 1957): 3.

151. Adam Goodheart, *1861: The Civil War Awakening* (New York: Alfred A. Knopf, 2011), 350.

152. Bayne, *Tad Lincoln's Father*, 30.

153. Bayne, *Tad Lincoln's Father*, 30-31.

154. Bayne, *Tad Lincoln's Father*, 31.

155. Peggy Robbins, "The Lincolns and Spiritualism," *Civil War Times Illustrated* (August 1976), 6.

156. "J.S. Hastings to Abraham Lincoln, Friday, August 9, 1861," Abraham Lincoln Papers at the Library of Congress, accessed November 3, 2011, http://memory.loc.gov/cgi-bin/query/r?ammem/mal:@field(DOCID+@lit(d1112300)).

157. "J.S. Hastings to Abraham Lincoln."

158. "J.S. Hastings to Abraham Lincoln, Saturday, September 7, 1861," Abraham Lincoln Papers at the Library of Congress, accessed November 3, 2011, http://memory.loc.gov/cgi-bin/query/P?mal:3:./temp/~ammem_G1Qx::.

159. "J.S. Hastings to Abraham Lincoln."

160. For more about Abraham Lincoln's relationship with Elmer Ellsworth and Edward D. Baker see Adam Goodheart, *1861: The Civil War Awakening* (New York: Alfred A. Knopf, 2011).

161. Donald, *Lincoln*, 107.

162. "I.B. Conklin to Abraham Lincoln, Saturday, December 28, 1861," Abraham Lincoln Papers at the Library of Congress, accessed November 3, 2011, http://memory.loc.gov/cgi-bin/query/r?ammem/mal:@field(DOCID+@lit(d1357400)). Note: the Library of Congress misidentifies J.B. Conklin as "I.B. Conklin."

163. "I.B. Conklin to Abraham Lincoln."

164. "I.B. Conklin to Abraham Lincoln."

165. Clinton, *Mrs. Lincoln*, 134.

166. Faust, *This Republic of Suffering*, 140.

167. *Washington Evening Star*, February 21, 1862.

168. Faust, *This Republic of Suffering*, 10.

169. Clinton, *Mrs. Lincoln*, 167.

170. Keckley, *Behind the Scenes*, 87.

171. Keckley, *Behind the Scenes*, 87.

172. Nettie Colburn Maynard, *Was Abraham Lincoln a Spiritualist? Or, Curious Revelations from the Life of a Trance Medium* (Chicago: The Progressive Thinker Publishing House, 1891, 1917), 40.

173. Donna McCreary, *Fashionable First Lady: The Victorian Wardrobe of Mary Lincoln* (Charleston: Lincoln Presentations, 2007), 79.

174. For more information about the Battle of Fredericksburg see George C. Rable, *Fredericksburg! Fredericksburg!* (Chapel Hill, NC: The University of North Carolina Press, 2002).

175. Catherine Clinton, *Mrs. Lincoln: A Life* (New York: Harper, 2009), 166. Doris Kearns Goodwin, *Team of Rivals: The Political Genius of Abraham Lincoln* (New York: Simon and Shuster, 2005), 420.

176. Keckley, *Behind the Scenes*, 88.

177. Jason Emerson, *The Madness of Mary Lincoln* (Carbondale: Southern University Press, 2007), 12. Emerson sees Mary Lincoln's depression following the deaths of Eddie and Willie as evidence that Mary suffered from a manic depressive bi-polar condition.

178. Baker, *Mary Todd Lincoln*, 210.

179. Keckley, *Behind the Scenes*, 101.

180. "The Latest News," *Chicago Daily Tribune*, February 27, 1862 (Courtesy of the Abraham Lincoln Presidential Library, Springfield, IL).

181. Baker, *Mary Todd Lincoln*, 219.

182. Noah Brooks, *Washington D.C. in Lincoln's Time* (Chicago: Quadrangle Books, 1971), 66.

183. See Jennifer Fleischner's *Mrs. Lincoln and Mrs. Keckly: The Remarkable Story of the Friendship between a First Lady and a Former Slave* (New York: Broadway Books, 2003) for more about Elizabeth Keckly's life as a slave.

184. Emerson, *The Madness of Mary Lincoln*, 204 n. 22.

185. Baker, *Mary Todd Lincoln*, 212. Fleischner, *Mrs. Lincoln and Mrs. Keckly*, 259.

186. Christopher Kiernan Coleman, *The Paranormal Presidency of Abraham Lincoln* (Atglen: Schiffer, Ltd., 2012), 105.

187. Bayne, *Tad Lincoln's Father*, 74-75.

188. Keckley, *Behind the Scenes*, 88.

189. Philip D. Jordan, "Skulls, Rappers, Ghosts, and Doctors," *Ohio State Archeological and Historical Quarterly*, vol. 53 (1944), 348.

190. E.W. Capron, *Modern Spiritualism its Facts and Fanaticisms its Consistencies and Contradictions* (Boston: Bela Marsh, 1855), 355.

191. Weisberg, *Talking to the Dead*, 162.

192. Anna L. Boyden, *Echoes from Hospital and White House: A Record of Mrs. Rebecca R. Pomroy's Experience in Wartime* (Boston: D. Lothrop & Co., 1884), 13-14.

193. Boyden, *Echoes of Hospital and White House*, 67-68.

194. Boyden, *Echoes of Hospital and White House*, 70.

195. Boyden, *Echoes of Hospital and White House*, 79.

196. Margaret Leech, *Reveille in Washington 1860-1865* (Alexandria: Time-Life Books Inc., 1962, 1980), 377.

197. Maynard, *Was Abraham Lincoln a Spiritualist?*, 6, 11.

198. Fayette Hall, *The Copperhead: Or, the Secret Political History of Our Civil War Unveiled* (New Haven: Fayette Hall, 1902), 48.

199. Hall, *The Copperhead*, 14.

200. Maynard, *Was Abraham Lincoln a Spiritualist?*, 19.

201. Maynard, *Was Abraham Lincoln a Spiritualist?*, 19.

202. Maynard, *Was Abraham Lincoln a Spiritualist?*, 20.

203. Maynard, *Was Abraham Lincoln a Spiritualist?*, 20.

204. Maynard, *Was Abraham Lincoln a Spiritualist?*, 22, 30.

205. Alfred Hunter, *The Washington and Georgetown Directory, Strangers' Guide-Book for Washington, and Congressional and Clerks' Register* (Washington, D.C.: Kirkwood and McGill, 1853), 102.

206. Benjamin Brown French, *Witness to the Young Republic: A Yankee's Journal, 1828-1870*, edited by Donald B. Cole and John J. McDonough (Hanover: University Press of New England, 1989), 247.

207. Maynard, *Was Abraham Lincoln a Spiritualist?*, 31.

208. Coleman, *The Paranormal Presidency of Abraham Lincoln*, 90.

209. Maynard, *Was Abraham Lincoln a Spiritualist?*, 38.

210. Maynard, *Was Abraham Lincoln a Spiritualist?*, 92.

211. Maynard, *Was Abraham Lincoln a Spiritualist?*, 38.

212. Maynard, *Was Abraham Lincoln a Spiritualist?*, 38.

213. Troy Taylor, *The Haunted President: The History, Haunting & Supernatural Life of Abraham Lincoln* (Decatur: Whitechapel Press, 2005, 2009), 60.

214. Daniel Mark Epstein, *The Lincolns: Portrait of a Marriage* (New York: Ballantine Books, 2008), 381.

215. Maynard, *Was Abraham Lincoln a Spiritualist?*, 38-39.

216. F.B. Carpenter, *The Inner Life of Abraham Lincoln: Six Months at the White House* (Lincoln, NE: University of Nebraska Press, 1995), 117.

217. Clinton, *Mrs. Lincoln*, 173.

218. Clinton, *Mrs. Lincoln*, 173.

219. Taylor, *The Haunted President*, 49.

220. Keckley, *Behind the Scenes*, 169. Goodwin, *Team of Rivals*, 423.

221. Goodwin, *Team of Rivals*, 482-483.

222. For more about the criticism Abraham Lincoln faced regarding the Emancipation Proclamation see William K. Klingaman, *Abraham Lincoln and the Road to Emancipation 1861-1865* (New York: Penguin Books, 2001) and Louis P. Masur, *Lincoln's Hundred Days: The Emancipation Proclamation and the War for the Union* (Cambridge: The Belknap Press of Harvard University Press, 2012).

223. Boyden, *Echoes of Hospital and White House*, 121-122.

224. Harry R. Rubenstein, *Abraham Lincoln: An Extraordinary Life* (Washington, D.C.: Smithsonian Books, 2008), 55.

225. Fayette Hall, *The Secret and Political History of the Rebellion: The Causes Leading Thereto, and the Effects, Showing How Abraham Lincoln Came to be President of the United States, Exposing the Secret Working and Conspiring of Those in Power, and the Motive and Purpose of Prolonging the War for Four Years!* (New Haven, CT: Fayette Hall, 1890), 21.

226. Hall, *Secret Political History* 8.

227. Hall, *Secret Political History* 27.

228. Simon P. Kase, *The Emancipation Proclamation: How, and by Whom, It was Given to Abraham Lincoln in 1861* (Philadelphia: S.P. Kase, n.d.), 14.

229. Kase, *The Emancipation Proclamation*, 15.

230. Kase, *The Emancipation Proclamation*, 15.

231. Hall, *Secret and Political History*, 22.

232. Hall, *Secret and Political History*, 23.

233. Kase, *The Emancipation Proclamation*, 16-21.

234. Hall, *Secret and Political History*, 23.

235. Kase, *The Emancipation Proclamation*, 22.

236. Hall, *Secret and Political History*, 21. Kase, *The Emancipation Proclamation*, 12-13.

237. Kase, *The Emancipation Proclamation*, 24.

238. Anonymous, *Old Abe's Jokes: Fresh from Abraham's Bosom* (New York: T.R. Dawley, 1864), 34.

239. Hall, *Secret and Political History*, 25. A gudgeon is slang for a person who is easily duped.

240. Hall, *Secret and Political History*, 25.

241. Hall, *Secret and Political History*, 25.

242. Hall, *The Copperhead*, 51.

243. Hall, *The Copperhead*, 48.

244. John C. Waugh, *One Man Great Enough: Abraham Lincoln's Road to the Civil War* (Boston: Mariner Books, 2007), 48.

245. Noah Brooks, "Personal Reminiscences of Lincoln," *Scribner's Monthly*, vol. 15, issue 4 (February 1878), 565.

246. Lydia Smith to Abraham Lincoln, Saturday, October 4, 1862,"Abraham Lincoln Papers at the Library of Congress, accessed November 3, 2011, http://memory.loc.gov/cgi-bin/query/r?ammem/mal:@field(DOCID+lit(d1886200).

247. "Lydia Smith to Abraham Lincoln."

248. Anonymous, *Old Abe's Jokes*, 30.

249. Maynard, *Was Abraham Lincoln a Spiritualist?*, 40.

250. Maynard, *Was Abraham Lincoln a Spiritualist?*, 40.

251. Maynard, *Was Abraham Lincoln a Spiritualist?*, 41.

252. Maynard, *Was Abraham Lincoln a Spiritualist?*, 41-42.

253. Anonymous, *Old Abe's Jokes*, 30-31.

254. Maynard, *Was Abraham Lincoln a Spiritualist?*, 42.

255. Jay Monaghan, "Was Abraham Lincoln Really a Spiritualist?" *The Journal of the Illinois State Historical Society*, vol. 34, no. 2 (June 1941), 218.

256. Monaghan, "Was Abraham Lincoln Really a Spiritualist?" 228.

257. William H. Herndon, "Letters from Lincoln's Old Partner," *Religio-Philosophical Journal*, December 12, 1885 (Courtesy of the Peabody Room, District of Columbia Public Library, Georgetown Neighborhood Branch, Washington, D.C.).

Donald, *"We Are Lincoln Men"*, 132.

Orville Hickman Browning, *The Diary of Orville Hickman Browning: Volume I, 1850-1864*, ed. Theodore Calvin Pease, (Springfield, IL: Illinois State Historical Library, 1925), 608-609.

258. Browning, *The Diary of Orville Hickman Browning*, 609.

259. See Ann Braude, *Radical Spirits: Spiritualism and Women's Rights in Nineteenth-Century America* (Bloomington: Indiana University Press, 1989, 2001).

260. "The Lincolns and Spiritualism," *Lincoln Lore*, April 15, 1946 (No. 888).

261. Nettie Colburn Maynard, *Was Abraham Lincoln a Spiritualist? Or, Curious Revelations from the Life of a Trance Medium* (Chicago: The Progressive Thinker Publishing House, 1891, 1917), 54.

262. Maynard, *Was Abraham Lincoln a Spiritualist?*, 48.

263. Fayette Hall, *The Copperhead: Or, the Secret Political History of Our Civil War Unveiled* (New Haven: Fayette Hall, 1902), 48.

266. Maynard, *Was Abraham Lincoln a Spiritualist?*, 48. Fayette Hall, *The Secret Political History of the War of the Rebellion: The Causes Leading Thereto, and the Effects, Showing How Abraham Lincoln Came to be President of the United States, Exposing the Secret Working and Conspiring of Those in Power, and the Motive and Purpose of Prolonging the War for Four Years!* (New Haven: Fayette Hall, 1890), 58.

267. Maynard, *Was Abraham Lincoln a Spiritualist?*, 48.

268. Maynard, *Was Abraham Lincoln a Spiritualist?*, 48.

269. Jay Monaghan, "Was Abraham Lincoln Really a Spiritualist?" *The Journal of the Illinois State Historical Society*, vol. 34, no. 2, (June 1941), 219.

270. Allen C. Guelzo, *Abraham Lincoln: Redeemer President* (Grand Rapids, MI: William B. Eerdmans Publishing Company, 1999), 38. Wayne Temple, *Abraham Lincoln: From Skeptic to Prophet* (Mahomet: Mayhaven Publishing, 1995), 5.

271. Maynard, *Was Abraham Lincoln a Spiritualist?*, 48-49.

272. Maynard, *Was Abraham Lincoln a Spiritualist?*, 50-51.

273. Maynard, *Was Abraham Lincoln a Spiritualist?*, 51.

274. Maynard, *Was Abraham Lincoln a Spiritualist?*, 53.

275. Troy Taylor, *Ghosts by Gaslight: The History & Mystery of the Spiritualists & the Ghost Hunters* (Decatur: Whitechapel Productions Press, 2007), 54.

276. Maynard, *Was Abraham Lincoln a Spiritualist?*, 53.

277. Maynard, *Was Abraham Lincoln a Spiritualist?*, 53.

278. Hall, *Secret and Political History*, 24.

279. See Jack Crawford, *The Poet Scout: Being a Selection of Incidental and Illustrative Verses and Songs* (San Francisco: H. Keller & Co., 1879), 197. Crawford recounts seeing President Abraham Lincoln chopping wood outside a hospital in Petersburg, VA in April 1865.

280. Noah Brooks, "Personal Reminiscences of Lincoln," *Scribner's Monthly*, (February 1878), 565.

281. Maynard, *Was Abraham Lincoln a Spiritualist?*, 53.

282. Cyrus Oliver Poole, "The Religious Convictions of Abraham Lincoln. A Study," *The Religio-Philosophical Journal*, November 28, 1885. (Courtesy of the Peabody Room, District of Columbia Public Library, Georgetown Neighborhood Branch, Washington, D.C.).

283. Poole, "The Religious Convictions of Abraham Lincoln."

284. Poole, "The Religious Convictions of Abraham Lincoln."

285. Catherine Clinton, *Mrs. Lincoln: A Life* (New York: Harper, 2009), 173.

286. Poole, "The Religious Convictions of Abraham Lincoln."

287. Poole, "The Religious Convictions of Abraham Lincoln."

288. Hall, *Secret and Political History*, 12.

289. Hall, *Secret and Political History*, 16.

290. Hall, *Secret and Political History*, 25.

291. Hall, *Secret and Political History*, 26.

292. Hall, *Secret and Political History*, 8.

293. Hall, *Secret and Political History*, 20.

294. Maynard, *Was Abraham Lincoln a Spiritualist?*, 54.

295. Maynard, *Was Abraham Lincoln a Spiritualist?*, 54.

296. Mitch Horowitz, *Occult America: The Secret History of How Mysticism Shaped Our Nation* (New York: Bantam Books, 2009), 59.

297. "Lincoln's Attendance at Spiritualistic Séance's," *Lincoln Lore*, no. 1499, (January 1963), 3.

298. Peggy Robbins, "The Lincolns and Spiritualism," *Civil War Times Illustrated* 15 (August 1976), 46.

299. "Lincoln's Attendance at Spiritualistic Séance's," 3.

300. "Lincoln's Attendance at Spiritualistic Séance's," 3.

301. "Lincoln's Attendance at Spiritualistic Séance's," 3-4.

302. "Lincoln's Attendance at Spiritualistic Séance's," 4.

303. "Lincoln's Attendance at Spiritualistic Séance's," 4.

304. "Lincoln's Attendance at Spiritualistic Séance's," 4.

305. Robbins, "The Lincolns and Spiritualism," 47.

306. David Quinn, *Interior Causes of the War: The Nation Demonized, and it's President a Spirit-Rapper* (New York: M. Doolady, 1863), 5.

307. Quinn, *Interior Causes of the War*, 94-95.

308. Quinn, *Interior Causes of the War*, 101.

309. J.H. Addison, "The Dark Séance Polka," (London: Metzler & Co., n.d.). (Courtesy of the Lincoln Memorial University Archives, Harrogate, TN).

310. T.E. Carrett and W.W. Rossington, "Spirit Rappings" (Boston: Oliver Ditson, 1853), Duke University Libraries Historic American Sheet Music, accessed January 24, 2013, http://library.duke.edu/rubenstein/scriptorium/sheetmusic/a/a85/a8564/.

311. J.H. Addison, "The Dark Séance Polka," (London: Metzler & Co., n.d.). (Courtesy of the Lincoln Memorial University Archives, Harrogate, TN).

312. "Lincoln's Attendance at Spiritualistic Séance's," *Lincoln Lore*, January 1963 (No. 1499), 1.

313. Maynard, *Was Abraham Lincoln a Spiritualist?*, 58.

314. Maynard, Was *Abraham Lincoln a Spiritualist?*, 58.

315. Maynard, *Was Abraham Lincoln a Spiritualist?*, 59.

316. Maynard, *Was Abraham Lincoln a Spiritualist?*, 59.

317. Maynard, *Was Abraham Lincoln a Spiritualist?*, 60.

318. Maynard, *Was Abraham Lincoln a Spiritualist?*, 60.

319. "John W. Edmonds to Abraham Lincoln, Monday, June 1, 1863," Abraham Lincoln Papers at the Library of Congress, accessed November 11, 2011, http://memory.loc.gove/cgi-bin/query/r?ammem/mal:@field(DOCID+lit(d2381000)).

320. "John W. Edmonds to Abraham Lincoln, Monday, June 1, 1863."

321. "John W. Edmonds to Abraham Lincoln."

322. David Herbert Donald, *"We Are Lincoln Men": Abraham Lincoln and His Friends* (New York: Simon and Schuster, 2003), 39.

323. Donald, *"We Are Lincoln Men"*, 60-62.

324. "Joshua F. Speed to Abraham Lincoln, Monday, October 26, 1863," Abraham Lincoln Papers at the Library of Congress, accessed November 3, 2011, http://memory.loc.gov/cgi-bin/query/r?ammem/mal:@field(DOCID+@lit(d2751800)).

325. Maynard, *Was Abraham Lincoln a Spiritualist?*, 69.

326. Maynard, *Was Abraham Lincoln a Spiritualist?*, 69-70.

327. Maynard, *Was Abraham Lincoln a Spiritualist?*, 68.

328. "Joshua Speed to Abraham Lincoln."

329. Maynard, *Was Abraham Lincoln a Spiritualist?*, 70.

330. Maynard, *Was Abraham Lincoln a Spiritualist?*, 72.

331. Maynard, *Was Abraham Lincoln a Spiritualist?*, 73.

333. Maynard, *Was Abraham Lincoln a Spiritualist?*, 58.

334. Maynard, *Was Abraham Lincoln a Spiritualist?*, 54.

335. Quinn, *Interior Causes of the War*, 104.

336. Noah Brooks, *Washington, D.C. in Lincoln's Time* (Chicago: Quadrangle Books, 1971), 66.

337. Brooks, *Washington, D.C. in Lincoln's Time*, 66.

338. Mansfield, *Lincoln's Battle with God*, 155.

339. Brooks, *Washington D.C. in Lincoln's Time*, 66-67.

340. Brooks, *Washington D.C. in Lincoln's Time*, 8-9.

341. Brooks, *Washington, D.C. in Lincoln's Time*, 67.

342. Thomas Coulson, *Joseph Henry: His Life and Work* (Princeton: Princeton University Press, 1950), 308.

343. Coulson, *Joseph Henry*, 308-309.

344. Brooks, *Washington, D.C. in Lincoln's Time*, 67.

345. Brooks, *Washington, D.C. in Lincoln's Time*, 67.

346. Brooks, *Washington, D.C. in Lincoln's Time*, 67.

347. Brooks, *Washington, D.C. in Lincoln's Time*, 68.

348. Brooks, *Washington, D.C. in Lincoln's Time*, 68.

349. Stephen Berry, *House of Abraham: Lincoln and the Todds, a Family Divided by War* (Boston: Houghton Mifflin Company, 2007), 151-152.

350. Alexander Todd, Mary Lincoln's favorite half-brother, joined the Confederate Army and died in the fall of 1863 during a skirmish near Baton Rouge, Louisiana. Upon hearing of her brother's death Mary Lincoln is said to have exclaimed, "Oh little Aleck, why had you to die?" Jean H. Baker, *Mary Todd Lincoln: A Biography* (New York: W.W. Norton & Company, 1987), 222-223.

351. Helm, *The True Story of Mary, Wife of* Lincoln,226-227.

352. Helm, *True Story of Mary*, 227.

353. "Edwin D. Morgan to Abraham Lincoln, Saturday, January 16, 1864," Abraham Lincoln Papers at the Library of Congress, accessed November 3, 2011, http://memory.loc.gov/cgi-bin/query/r?ammem/mal:@field (DOCID+@lit(d2953900)).

354. Roy Basler, *The Collected Works of Abraham Lincoln, Volume VII* (Springfield: The Abraham Lincoln Association, 1953), 133.

355. Tom Wheeler, *Mr. Lincoln's T-Mail: How President Lincoln Used the Telegraph to Win the Civil War* (New York: Collins, 2006), 108.

356. Maynard, *Was Abraham Lincoln a Spiritualist?*, 74.

357. Coleman, *The Paranormal Presidency of Abraham Lincoln*, 98.

358. Maynard, *Was Abraham Lincoln a Spiritualist?*, 74.

359. Maynard, *Was Abraham Lincoln a Spiritualist?*, 74.

360. Maynard, *Was Abraham Lincoln a Spiritualist?*, 74-75.

361. Maynard, *Was Abraham Lincoln a Spiritualist?*, 75.

362. Maynard, *Was Abraham Lincoln a Spiritualist?*, 76.

363. Maynard, *Was Abraham Lincoln a Spiritualist?*, 76-78.

364. Maynard, *Was Abraham Lincoln a Spiritualist?*, xxiii.

365. Maynard, *Was Abraham Lincoln a Spiritualist?*, 77.

366. Maynard, *Was Abraham Lincoln a Spiritualist?*, 80.

367. Donald, *"We Are Lincoln Men"*, 68-69.

368. Thomas M. Schwartz, *Mary Todd Lincoln: First Lady of Controversy* (Springfield, IL: Abraham Lincoln Presidential Library Foundation, 2007), 43.

369. Maynard, *Was Abraham Lincoln a Spiritualist?*, xvii.

370. Maynard, *Was Abraham Lincoln a Spiritualist?*, 92.

371. Maynard, *Was Abraham Lincoln a Spiritualist?*, 92.

372. Maynard, *Was Abraham Lincoln a Spiritualist?*, 101.

373. Maynard, *Was Abraham Lincoln a Spiritualist?*, 101-102.

374. Maynard, *Was Abraham Lincoln a Spiritualist?*, 102.

375. Ronald C. White, Jr., *A. Lincoln: A Biography* (New York: Random House, 2009), 639.

376. Doris Kearns Goodwin, *Team of Rivals: The Political Genius of Abraham Lincoln* (New York: Simon & Shuster, 2005), 666.

377. "R.A. Beck to Abraham Lincoln, November-December 1864," Abraham Lincoln Papers at the Library of Congress, accessed November 3, 2011, http://memory.loc.gov/cgi-bin/query/r?ammem/mal:@field(DOCID+@lit(d3884700)).

378. "R.A. Beck to Abraham Lincoln."

379. "R.A. Beck to Abraham Lincoln."

380. Prof. W.H. Chaney, "Was He a Spiritualist? Reminiscences of President Lincoln," *The Religio-Philosophical Journal*, January 16, 1886. (Courtesy of the Library of Congress, Washington, D.C.).

381. Prof. W.H. Chaney, "Was He a Spiritualist? Reminiscences of President Lincoln."

382. Prof. W.H. Chaney, "Was He a Spiritualist? Reminiscences of President Lincoln."

383. "Mrs. M.A. Laurie to Abraham Lincoln, Monday, December 19, 1864," Abraham Lincoln Papers at the Library of Congress, accessed January 14, 2013, http://memory.loc.gov/cgi-bin/ampage.

384. Maynard, *Was Abraham Lincoln a Spiritualist?*, 113.

385. Maynard, *Was Abraham Lincoln a Spiritualist?*, 114.

386. Gideon Welles and Edgar Thaddeus Welles, *Diary of Gideon Welles, Secretary of the Navy under Lincoln and Johnson, Volume II: April 1, 1864-December 31, 1866* (Boston: Houghton Mifflin Company, 1911), 282-283.

387. Welles and Welles, *Diary of Gideon Welles*, 283.

388. Welles and Welles, *Diary of Gideon Welles*, 283.

389. Nettie Colburn Maynard, *Was Abraham Lincoln a Spiritualist? Or, Curious Revelations from the Life of a Trance Medium* (Chicago: The Progressive Thinker Publishing House, 1891, 1917), 109.

390. Maynard, *Was Abraham Lincoln a Spiritualist?*, 109.

391. Maynard, *Was Abraham Lincoln a Spiritualist?*, 110.

392. Maynard, *Was Abraham Lincoln a Spiritualist?*, 110-111.

393. Coleman, *The Paranormal Presidency of Abraham Lincoln*, 118-199.

394. Margarita Spalding Gerry, *Through Five Administrations: Reminiscences of Colonel William H. Crook, Body-Guard to President Lincoln* (New York: Harper & Brothers, 1910), 76.

395. Catherine Clinton, *Mrs. Lincoln: A Life* (New York: Harper, 2009), 3.

396. Gerry, *Through Five* Administrations, 69-70.

397. Justin G. Turner and Linda Levitt Turner, *Mary Todd Lincoln: Her Life and Letters* (New York: Alfred A. Knopf, 1972), 525.

398. Elizabeth Stuart Phelps, *The Gates Ajar* (Boston: Fields, Osgood, & Co., 1868, 1869), 54.

399. Schwartz, *Mary Todd* Lincoln, 75.

400. Phelps, *The Gates Ajar*, 83.

401. Turner and Turner, *Mary Todd Lincoln: Her Life and Letters*, 579-580.

402. Baker, *Mary Todd Lincoln*, 308.

403. Louis Kaplan, *The Strange Case of William Mumler Spirit Photographer* (Minneapolis: University of Minnesota Press, 2008), 19.

404. Kaplan, *The Strange Case of William Mumler Spirit Photographer*, 81-82.

405. Kaplan, *The Strange Case of William Mumler Spirit Photographer*, 92.

406. Kaplan, *The Strange Case of William Mumler Spirit Photographer*, 93.

407. Kaplan, *The Strange Case of William Mumler Spirit Photographer*, 93.

408. Emerson, *The Madness of Mary Lincoln*, 43.

409. Emerson, *The Madness of Mary Lincoln*, 61.

410. Baker, *Mary Todd Lincoln*, 368.

411. J.B. McClure, editor, *Anecdotes and Stories of Abraham Lincoln* (Mechanicsburg, PA: Stackpole Books, 2006), 204-206.

412. Coleman, *The Paranormal Presidency of Abraham Lincoln*, 91.

413. Kase, *The Emancipation Proclamation: How, and by Whom, It was Given to Abraham Lincoln in 1861*, 25.

414. "The Lincolns and Spiritualism," *Lincoln Lore*, no. 888 (April 15, 1946), 1.

415. "The Lincolns and Spiritualism," *Lincoln Lore*, no. 888 (April 15, 1946), 1.

416. Jeff Belanger, *Who's Haunting the White House? The President's Mansion and the Ghosts who Live There* (New York: Sterling Children's Books, 2008).

417. *Gore Vidal's Lincoln*, directed by Lamont Johnson (1988; Los Angeles, CA: Platinum Disk, 2004), DVD.

418. James Still, *The Heavens Are Hung in Black* (Woodstock: Dramatic Publishing, 2012), 20.

419. *These Old Broads*, directed by Matthew Diamond (2000; Culver City, CA: Sony Pictures Home Entertainment, 2009), DVD.

420. *American Dad*, "Black Mystery Month," directed by Brent Woods (2007, Los Angeles, CA: 20th Century Fox, 2008), DVD.

Bibliography

Primary Source

Addison, J.H. "The Dark Séance Polka." London: Metzler & Co., n.d.
Lincoln Memorial University Archives, Harrogate, TN.

Anonymous. *Old Abe's Jokes: Fresh from Abraham's Bosom.* New York: T.R. Dawley, 1864.

Basler, Roy P. *The Collected Works of Abraham Lincoln, Volume VII.* The Abraham Lincoln Association, 1953.

Bayne, Julia Taft. *Tad's Lincoln's Father.* Lincoln: University of Nebraska Press, 2001.

"R.A. Beck to Abraham Lincoln, November-December 1864." Abraham Lincoln Papers at the Library of Congress. http://memory.loc.gov/cgi-bin/query/r?ammem/mal:@field(DOCID+@lit(d3884700)) (accessed November 3, 2011).

Brooks, Noah. "Recollections of Abraham Lincoln," *Harper's New Monthly Magazine* (July 1865): 222-230.

Brooks, Noah. "Personal Reminiscences of Lincoln," *Scriber's Monthly*, vol. 15, issue 4 (February 1878): 561-569.

Brooks, Noah. *Washington D.C. in Lincoln's Time.* Chicago: Quadrangle Books, 1971.

Browning, Orville Hickman. *The Diary of Orville Hickman Browning: Volume I, 1850-1864.* Springfield: Illinois State Historical Library, 1925.

Capron, E.W. *Modern Spiritualism its Facts and Fanaticisms its Consistencies and Contradictions.* Boston: Bela Marsh, 1855.

Carpenter, F.B. *The Inner Life of Abraham Lincoln: Six Months at the White House.* Lincoln: University of Nebraska Press, 1995.

Carrett, T.E. and W.W. Rossington. "Spirit Rappings." Boston: Oliver Ditson, 1853. Duke University Libraries Historic American Sheet Music. http://library.duke.edu/rubenstein/scriptorium/sheetmusic/a/a85/a8564/ (accessed January 24, 2013).

Chaney, Prof. W.H. "Was He a Spiritualist? Reminisces of President Lincoln," *The Religio-Philosophical Journal*, January 16, 1886. Library of Congress, Washington, D.C.

Crawford, Jack. *The Poet Scout: Being a Selection of Incidental and Illustrative Verses and Songs.* San Francisco: H. Keller & Co. 1879.

Crawford, Jack. *The Poet Scout: Being a Selection of Incidental and Illustrative Verses and Songs*. San Francisco: H. Keller & Co. 1879.

"I.B. Conklin to Abraham Lincoln, Saturday, December 28, 1861," Abraham Lincoln Papers at the Library of Congress. http://memory.loc.gov/cgi-bin/query/r?ammem/mal:@field (DOCID+@lit(d1357400)) (accessed November 3, 2011).

Daily Illinois State Journal, August 19, 1851. Sangamon Valley Collection, Lincoln Library, Springfield, IL.

Daily Illinois State Journal, March 3, 1858. Sangamon Valley Collection, Lincoln Library, Springfield, IL.

Daily Illinois State Journal, October 20, 1858. Sangamon Valley Collection, Lincoln Library, Springfield, IL.

Daily Illinois State Journal, November 17, 1858. Sangamon Valley Collection, Lincoln Library, Springfield, IL.

Daily Illinois State Journal, December 21, 1858. Sangamon Valley Collection, Lincoln Library, Springfield, IL.

Daily Illinois State Journal, December 15, 1859. Sangamon Valley Collection, Lincoln Library, Springfield, IL.

"John W. Edmonds to Abraham Lincoln, Monday, June 1, 1863," Abraham Lincoln Papers at the Library of Congress. http://memory.loc.gov/cgi-bin/query/r?ammem/mal:@field(DOCID+lit (d2381000)) (accessed November 11, 2011).

French, Benjamin Brown. *Witness to the Young Republic: A Yankee's Journal, 1828-1870*. Hanover: University Press of New England, 1989.

"G.A. A Wide Awake to Abraham Lincoln, Tuesday, December 11, 1860," Abraham Lincoln Papers at the Library of Congress. http://memory.loc.gov/cgi-bin/query/r?ammem/mal:@field (DOCID+@lit(do4977700)) (accessed November 3, 2011).

Gerry, Margarita Spalding Gerry. *Through Five Administrations: Reminiscences of Colonel William H. Crook, Body-Guard to President Lincoln*. New York: Harper & Brothers, 1910.

Hall, Fayette. *The Copperhead: Or, the Secret Political History of Our Civil War Unveiled*. New Haven: Fayette Hall, 1902.

Hall, Fayette. *The Secret and Political History of the Rebellion: The Causes Leading Thereto, and the Effects, Showing How Abraham Lincoln Came to be President of the United States, Exposing the Secret Working and Conspiring of Those in Power, and the Motive and Purpose of Prolonging the War for Four Years!* New Haven: Fayette Hall, 1890.

Hardinge, Emma. *Modern American Spiritualism: A Twenty Years' Record of the Communion between Earth and the World of the Spirits*. New York: Emma Hardinge, 1870.

"J.S. Hastings to Abraham Lincoln, Friday, August 9, 1861," Abraham Lincoln Papers at the Library of Congress. http://memory.loc.gov/cgi-bin/query/r?ammem/mal:@field(DOCID+lit(d1112300)) (accessed November 3, 2011).

"J.S. Hastings to Abraham Lincoln, Saturday, September 7, 1861," Abraham Lincoln Papers at the Library of Congress. http://memory.loc.gov/cgi-bin/query/P?mal:3:./temp/~ammem_G1Qx:: (accessed November 3, 2011).

Herndon, William H. "Letters from Lincoln's Old Partner," *Religio-Philosophical Journal*, December 12, 1885. Peabody Room, District of Columbia Public Library, Georgetown Neighborhood Branch, Washington, D.C.

Hunter, Alfred. *The Washington and Georgetown Directory, Strangers' Guide-Book for Washington, and Congressional and Clerks' Register*. Washington, D.C.: Kirkwood and McGill, 1853.

Kase, Simon P. *The Emancipation Proclamation: How, and by Whom, It was Given to Abraham Lincoln in 1861*. Philadelphia: S.P. Kase, n.d.

Keckley, Elizabeth. *Behind the Scenes: Formerly a Slave, But More Recently Modiste, and Friend to Mrs. Lincoln Or, Thirty Years a Slave and Four Years in the White House*. Chicago: The Lakeside Press, 1868, 1998.

"The Latest News," *Chicago Daily Tribune*, February 27, 1862. Abraham Lincoln Presidential Library, Springfield, IL.

"Mrs. M.A. Laurie to Abraham Lincoln, Monday, December 19, 1864." Abraham Lincoln Papers at the Library of Congress. http://memory.loc.gov/cgi-bin/ampage (accessed January 14, 2013).

Maynard, Nettie Colburn. *Was Abraham Lincoln a Spiritualist? Or, Curious Revelations from the Life of a Trance Medium*. Chicago: The Progressive Thinker Publishing House, 1891, 1917.

McClure, J.B. *Anecdotes and Stories of Abraham Lincoln*. Mechanicsburg: Stackpole Books, 2006).

"Edwin D. Morgan to Abraham Lincoln, Saturday, January 16, 1864." Abraham Lincoln Papers at the Library of Congress. http://memory.loc.gov/cgi-bin/query/r?ammem/mal:@field(DOCID+lit(d2953900)) (accessed November 3, 2011).

Phelps, Elizabeth Stuart. *The Gates Ajar*. Boston: Fields, Osgood, & Co., 1868, 1869.

Poole, Cyrus Oliver. "The Religious Convictions of Abraham Lincoln: A Study," *The Religio-Philosophical Journal*, November 28, 1885. Peabody Room, District of Columbia Public Library, Georgetown Neighborhood Branch, Washington, D.C.

Quinn, David. *Interior Causes of the War: The Nation Demonized, and it's President a Spirit-Rapper.* New York: M. Doolady, 1863.

"The President Elect A Spiritualist," *The Waukesha Freeman*, March 12, 1861.

Richmond, Thomas. *God Dealing With Slavery.* Chicago: Religio-Philosophical Publishing House, 1870.

"Rutland Reform Convention," *The Liberator*, July 2, 1858.

Sandburg, Carl. *Lincoln's Devotional.* New York: Henry Holt Company, 1995.

Schwartz, Thomas F. and Kim M. Bauer. "Unpublished Mary Todd Lincoln," *Journal of the Abraham Lincoln Association* (Summer 1996): 1-21.

"Lydia Smith to Abraham Lincoln, Saturday, October 4, 1862," Abraham Lincoln Papers at the Library of Congress. http://memory.loc.gov/cgi-bin/query/r?ammem/mal:@field(DOCID+lit (d1886200) (accessed November 3, 2011).

"Joshua F. Speed to Abraham Lincoln, Monday, October 26, 1863." Abraham Lincoln Papers at the Library of Congress. http://memory.loc.gov/cgi-bin/query/r?ammem/mal:@field (DOCID+@lit(d2751800)) (accessed November 3, 2011).

Temple, Wayne C. "Herndon on Lincoln: An Unknown Interview with a List of Books in the Lincoln & Herndon Law Office," *Journal of the Illinois State Historical Society*, vol. 98, no. 1/2: 34-50.

Turner, Justin G. and Linda Levitt Turner. *Mary Todd Lincoln: Her Life and Letters.* New York: Alfred A. Knopf, 1972.

Washington Evening Star, February 21, 1862.

Welles, Gideon and Edgar Thaddeus Welles. *Diary of Gideon Welles, Secretary of the Navy under Lincoln and Johnson, Volume II: April 1, 1864-December 31, 1866.* Boston: Houghton Mifflin Company, 1911.

Young, Dwight and Margaret Johnson. *Dear First Lady: Letters to the White House from the Collections of the Library of Congress and National Archives.* Washington, D.C.: National Geographic, 2008.

Secondary Sources

Albanese, Catherine L. *A Republic of Mind and Spirit: A Cultural History of American Metaphysical Religion*. Princeton: Princeton University Press, 1999.

Allgor, Catherine. *Parlor Politics: In Which the Ladies of Washington Help Build a City and a Government*. Charlottesville: University Press of Virginia, 2000.

Alter, Emily. "The Spiritualist Movement and its Advancement of the Nineteenth Century Women's Movement," *The Concord Review*, (2001): 167-192.

American Dad, "Black Mystery Month." Directed by Brent Woods. 2007. Los Angeles, CA: 20th Century Fox, 2008. DVD.

"Astrological Predictions: The Presidential Campaign of 1860," *Lincoln Lore*, no. 1433 (July 1957): 1-3.

Baker, Jean H. *Mary Todd Lincoln*. New York: W.W. Norton and Company, 1987.

Belanger, Jeff. *Who's Haunting the White House? The President's Mansion and the Ghosts who Live There*. New York: Sterling Children's Books, 2008.

Berkin, Carol. *Civil War Wives: The Lives & Times of Angelina Grimké Weld, Varina Howell Davis & Julia Dent Grant*. New York: Alfred A. Knopf, 2009.

Berry, Stephen. *House of Abraham: Lincoln and the Todds, a Family Divided by War*. New York Houghton Mifflin Harcourt, 2007.

Boyden, Anna L. *Echoes from Hospital and White House: A Record of Mrs. Rebecca R. Pomroy's Experience in Wartime*. Boston: D. Lothrop & Co., 1884.

Braude, Ann. *Radical Spirits: Spiritualism and Women's Rights in Nineteenth-Century America*. Bloomington: Indiana University Press, 1989, 2001.

Brue, Sandra, Mike Capps, and Timothy P. Townsend. *Abraham Lincoln: A Living Legacy: A Guide to Three Abraham Lincoln National Park Sites*. Virginia Beach: The Donning Company Publishers, 2008.

Campanella, Richard. *Lincoln in New Orleans: The 1828-1831 Flatboat Voyages and Their Place in History*. Lafayette: University of Louisiana at Lafayette Press, 2010.

Chadwick, Bruce. *Lincoln for President: An Unlikely Candidate, an Audacious Strategy, and the Victory No One Saw Coming.* Naperville: Sourcebooks, Inc., 2009.

Clinton, Catherine. *Mrs. Lincoln: A Life.* New York: Harper, 2009.

Coleman, Christopher Kiernan. *The Paranormal Presidency of Abraham Lincoln.* Atglen, PA: Schiffer Publishing, Ltd., 2012.

Coulson, Thomas. *Joseph Henry: His Life and Work.* Princeton: Princeton University Press, 1950.

Cooper, William J. *We Have the War Upon Us: The Onset of the Civil War, November 1860-April 1861.* New York: Alfred A. Knopf, 2012.

Cox, Robert S. *Body and Soul: A Sympathetic History of Spiritualism.* Charlottesville: University of Virginia Press, 2003.

Donald, David Herbert. *Lincoln.* New York: Simon & Schuster, 1995.

Donald, David Herbert. *Lincoln at Home: Two Glimpses of Abraham Lincoln's Domestic Life.* Washington, D.C.: White House Historical Association, 1999.

Donald, David Herbert. *"We Are Lincoln Men": Abraham Lincoln and His Friends.* New York: Simon & Schuster, 2003.

Emerson, Jason. *The Madness of Mary Lincoln.* Carbondale: Southern Illinois University Press, 2007.

Epstein, Daniel Mark. *The Lincolns: Portrait of a Marriage.* New York: Ballantine Books, 2008.

Faust, Drew Gilpin. *This Republic of Suffering: Death and the American Civil War.* New York: Alfred A. Knopf, 2008.

Fleischner, Jennifer. *Mrs. Lincoln and Mrs. Keckly: The Remarkable Story of the Friendship between a First Lady and a Former Slave.* New York: Broadway Books, 2003.

Goldberg, Vicki. *The White House: The President's Home in Photographs and History.* New York: Little, Brown and Company, 2011.

Gollaher, David L. *Voice for the Mad: The Life of Dorothea Dix.* New York: The Free Press, 1995.

Goodheart, Adam. *1861: The Civil War Awakening.* New York: Alfred A. Knopf, 2011.

Goodwin, Doris Kearns. *Teams of Rivals: The Political Genius of Abraham Lincoln.* New York: Simon and Shuster, 2005.

Gore Vidal's Lincoln. Directed by Lamont Johnson. 1988. Los Angeles, CA: Platinum Disk, 2004. DVD.

Guelzo, Allen C. *Abraham Lincoln: Redeemer President.* Grand Rapids: William B. Eerdmans Publishing Company, 1999.

Helm, Katherine. *The True Story of Mary, Wife of Lincoln: Containing the Recollections of Mary Lincoln's Sister Emilie (Mrs. Ben Hardin Helm), Extracts from Her War-Time Diary, Numerous Letters and Other Documents Now First Published.* New York: Harper and Brothers Publishing, 1928.

Holt, Michael F. *Franklin Pierce.* New York: Times Books, 2010.

Holzer, Harold. *Lincoln President-Elect: Abraham Lincoln and the Great Secession Winter 1860-1861.* New York: Simon & Schuster, 2008.

Horowitz, Mitch. *Occult America: The Secret History of How Mysticism Shaped Our Nation.* New York: Bantam Books, 2009.

Jordan, Philip D. "Skulls, Rappers, Ghosts, and Doctors," *Ohio State Archeological and Historical Quarterly*, vol. 53 (1944): 339-354.

Johnson, Paul E. and Sean Wilentz. *The Kingdom of Matthias: A Story of Sex and Salvation in 19th-Century America.* New York: Oxford University Press, 1994.

Kaplan, Louis. *The Strange Case of William Mumler Spirit Photographer.* Minneapolis: University of Minnesota Press, 2008.

Klingaman, William K. *Abraham Lincoln and the Road to Emancipation 1861-1865.* New York: Penguin Books, 2001.

Leech, Margaret. *Reveille in Washington 1860-1865.* Alexandria: Time-Life Books Inc., 1941, 1962, 1980.

"Lincoln's Attendance at Spiritualistic Séances: Part One," *Lincoln Lore*, no. 1499 (January 1963): 1-4.

"Lincoln's Attendance at Spiritualistic Séances: Part Two," *Lincoln Lore*, no. 1500 (February 1963): 1-3.

"The Lincolns and Spiritualism," *Lincoln Lore*, no. 888 (April 15, 1946): 1.

Mansfield, Stephen. *Lincoln's Battle with God: A President's Struggle with Faith and What it Meant for America.* Nashville: Thomas Nelson, 2012.

Marten, James. *Children for the Union: The War Spirit on the Northern Home Front.* Chicago: Ivan R. Dee, 2004.

Martinez, Susan B. *The Paranormal Presidency of Abraham Lincoln.* Franklin Lakes: New Page Books, 2009.

Masur, Louis P. *Lincoln's Hundred Days: The Emancipation Proclamation and the War for the Union.* Cambridge: The Belknap Press of Harvard University Press, 2012.

McCreary, Donna. *Fashionable First Lady: The Victorian Wardrobe of Mary Lincoln.* Charleston: Lincoln Presentation, 2007).

Monaghan, Jay. "Was Abraham Lincoln Really a Spiritualist?" *Journal of the Illinois State Historical Society*, vol. 34, no. 2 (June 1941): 209-232.

Nelson, Geoffrey K. *Spiritualism and Society*. New York: Schocken Books, 1969.

Nickell, Joe. "Paranormal Lincoln," *Skeptical Inquirer*, vol. 23 (May/June 1999). http://www.csicop.org/si/show/paranormal_lincoln/ (accessed January 31, 2013).

Ostendorf, Lloyd. *The Photographs of Mary Todd Lincoln*. Springfield: Illinois State Historical Society, 1969.

Peterson, Merrill D. *Lincoln in American Memory*. New York: Oxford University Press, 1994.

Rable, George C. *Fredericksburg! Fredericksburg!* Chapel Hill: The University of North Carolina Press, 2002.

Raboteau, Albert J. *Slave Religion: The "Invisible Institution" in the Antebellum South*. Oxford: Oxford University Press.

Reynolds, David S. *Mightier than the Sword: Uncle Tom's Cabin and the Battle for America*. New York: W.W. Norton & Company, 2011.

Robbins, Peggy. "The Lincolns and Spiritualism," *Civil War Times Illustrated* (August 1976): 4-10, 46-47.

Rubenstein, Harry R. *Abraham Lincoln: An Extraordinary Life*. Washington, D.C.: Smithsonian Books, 2008.

Schwartz, Thomas F, *Mary Todd Lincoln: First Lady of Controversy*. Springfield: Abraham Lincoln Presidential Library Foundation, 2007.

Stashower, Daniel. *The Hour of Peril: The Secret Plot to Murder Lincoln before the Civil War*. New York: Minotaur Books, 2013.

Still, James. *The Heavens Are Hung in Black*. Woodstock: Dramatic Publishing, 2012.

Stone, Irving. "Mary Todd Lincoln: A Final Judgment?" Springfield: Abraham Lincoln Association, 1973.

Taylor, Troy. *Ghosts by Gaslight: The History & Mystery of the Spiritualists & the Ghost Hunters*. Decatur: Whitechapel Production Press, 2007.

Taylor, Troy. *The Haunted President: The History, Hauntings & Supernatural Life of Abraham Lincoln*. Decatur: Whitechapel Press, 2005, 2009.

Taves, Ann. *Fits, Trances, and Visions: Experiencing Religion and Explaining Experience from Wesley to James*. Princeton: Princeton University Press, 1999.

Temple, Wayne C. *Abraham Lincoln: From Skeptic to Prophet*. Mahomet: Mayhaven Publishing, 1995.

These Old Broads. Directed by Matthew Diamond. 2000. Culver City, CA: Sony Pictures Home Entertainment, 2009. DVD.

Thomas, Benjamin P. *Abraham Lincoln: A Biography*. New York: The Modern Library, 1952, 1968.

Thomas, Benjamin P. *Lincoln's New Salem*. Carbondale: Southern Illinois University Press, 1954, 1988.

Waugh, John C. *One Man Great Enough: Abraham Lincoln's Road to the Civil War*. Boston: Mariner Books, 2007.

Weisberg, Barbara. *Talking to the Dead: Katie and Maggie Fox and the Rise of Spiritualism*. San Francisco: HarperSanFrancisco, 2004.

White, Ronald C. Jr. *A. Lincoln: A Biography*. New York: Random House, 2009.

Wheeler, Tom. *Mr. Lincoln's T-Mail: How President Lincoln Used the Telegraph to Win the Civil War*. New York: Collins, 2006.

Winkle, Kenneth J. *Abraham and Mary Lincoln*. Carbondale: Southern Illinois University Press, 2011.

ABOUT THE AUTHOR

Michelle L. Hamilton earned her master's degree in history from San Diego State University in 2013. Her work can be seen in the 2011 and 2013 *The Citizen's Companion*. A lifelong student of history, Hamilton has worked as a docent at the Whaley House Museum in Old Town San Diego from 2001 until 2006. She has been a Civil War living historian for the past ten years participating in Civil War living history events around California.

You can follow her at her blog:
http://michelle-hamilton.blogspot.com.